LIVING UPROOTED

LIVING UPROOTED

Encouragement for the Missionary Wife

MARI EYGABROAD

Published by Redemption Press, PO Box 427, Enumclaw, WA 98022.
Toll-Free (844) 2REDEEM (273-3336)

Redemption Press is honored to present this title in partnership with the author. The views expressed or implied in this work are those of the author. Redemption Press provides our imprint seal representing design excellence, creative content, and high-quality production.

The author has tried to recreate events, locales, and conversations from memories of them. In order to maintain their anonymity, in some instances the names of individuals, some identifying characteristics, and some details may have been changed, such as physical properties, occupations, and places of residence.

Unless otherwise indicated, all Scripture quotations are from the ESV® Bible (The Holy Bible, English Standard Version®), Copyright © 2001 by Crossway, a publishing ministry of Good News Publishers. Used by permission. All rights reserved.

Scripture quotations marked (NIV) are taken from the Holy Bible, New International Version®, NIV®. Copyright © 1973, 1978, 1984, 2011 by Biblica, Inc.™ Used by permission of Zondervan. All rights reserved worldwide. www.zondervan.com. The "NIV" and "New International Version" are trademarks registered in the United States Patent and Trademark Office by Biblica, Inc.™

Scripture quotations marked (KJV) are taken from the King James Version, public domain.

Portions of Scriptures have been italicized by the author to provide emphasis not specified in the original language or in the quoted translation. The author's intent is to enhance the reader's understanding.

ISBN 13: 978-1-64645-544-7 (Paperback)
978-1-64645-546-1 (ePub)
978-1-64645-545-4 (Mobi)

Library of Congress Catalog Card Number: 2021924712

For Jesus, who is my Lord and Savior; my husband, Bryan, my rock and my anchor; and our children: Matthias, Hope, Joy, Adia, and Isabella. Matthias, my firstborn son, you will forever be my rough-and-tumble baby boy! My angel babies—Hope (eight weeks), Joy (twelve weeks), Adia (thirty-six weeks)—gone too soon. Isabella, daughter of my heart, you've blessed our family with your spunk and sass! You can do all things through Christ (Philippians 4:13).

Table of Contents

Foreword

I'LL NEVER FORGET MY FIRST few weeks of missionary life in Indonesia.

Sweat poured from my body. My baby girl was covered in heat rash. Our family was weak after a bout of intestinal illness. The mosque call to prayer seemed to blare at us from all directions at all times of the day and night.

People babbled at us in a language that seemed incomprehensible. I struggled to pull together even the simplest of meals.

I remember watching planes take off from the local airport, wishing I could be on one of them, heading back to America, and away from this confusing world where everything felt upside down.

Is this what I signed up for, Lord? I remember praying. *Is this what you called me to?*

Thankfully, I didn't get on one of those planes. We dug in, did the hard work of learning the language and culture, and learned to deal with the heat. I learned to make a decent meal. Even the mosque call became a normal part of the background noise of our lives.

Over time, the foreign became familiar. For seventeen years, our family lived and served in Indonesia, pouring our hearts and souls into loving others well through our ministry. Along the way, I was helped by many sisters in Christ—fellow missionary wives—who were integral to my success. These women showed me how to shop at the market, shared tips on treating malaria, went with me to doctor's appointments, celebrated holidays together, cried with me during discouraging times, and prayed with me.

Churches in America sometimes put missionaries on pedestals, treating us like Christian royalty. While this kind of thinking is wrong, I do believe that missionary wives possess a certain tenacity and grit that sets them apart. The missionary wives I have known through the years make me think of the quote about the dancer, Ginger Rogers, who "did everything Fred Astaire did, but backwards and in high heels." Swap out flip-flops for the high heels, and it's about right.

Looking back on my early days overseas, I wish I had a book like this as a resource. Mari Eygabroad's story is unique, but also reflective of the experiences of missionary wives serving around the world.

Mari and I serve with the same organization, Mission Aviation Fellowship, and while we served in vastly different countries, our experiences were remarkably similar.

Her lesson of "adapt, alter, and adjust" will surely resonate with any who has served overseas, a life that demands flexibility. From support raising to processing loss to setting up a new home, Mari offers practical advice for the missionary spouse, while also weaving in her own story of following God's call to a life overseas.

Her chapter on spiritual warfare especially impacted me, as it was something I had never experienced in such a tangible way until we lived on a small island in Indonesia. Mari's story of God's protection and deliverance during times of spiritual attack is a reminder of the vital importance of prayer every step of the way.

The missionary life is a journey with God, a journey of growth and trust in the One who calls us. It's a life of challenges and struggles, but also of joy and blessing.

Whether you are contemplating missions, actively preparing to serve cross culturally, or just have a desire to better understand the life of a missionary wife, this insightful book will encourage you with its uplifting story of finding God's grace while living uprooted.

Natalie Holsten
Mission Aviation Fellowship

Living Uprooted - Thanks and Acknowledgments

SOME SAY WRITING IS A lonely endeavor. While many times I was alone while I was writing, I was never alone through the process. I owe many thanks to so many people who have supported me through this process.

I would like to thank my family. First, my husband, Bryan, for allowing me to use him as my sounding board, my story bank, my fact-checker, and first eyes editing to get this book written! Thank you for continually encouraging me and pushing me to keep going. Thanks to our son, Matthias, and our daughter, Isabella, for giving me the time and space to follow my dream of writing.

Thanks to my early readers and friends, Karen Adams, Amanda Honaker, Kathleen Martin, Emily Robbert, Jill Sanders, and Nikki Simpson, for giving open, honest feedback and input and contributing ideas and encouragement to incorporate into my book.

Many thanks to my content editor, Melanie Chitwood, Harvest House author of *What a Husband Needs from His Wife*, writer, writing coach, and editor at www.melanieschitwood.com for walking me through my entire manuscript and for her sharp editing skills, recommendations, prayers, and encouragement.

Thanks to my Compel critique group, Nancy, Darla, Britney, Brooke, Jessica, Mistie, Samantha, Susan, and Tracy, for their honest feedback on my work as I was getting started.

Thanks to the Flourish Writer's community for your support and encouragement to keep going, especially when I felt like giving up.

Thanks to my publishing team at Redemption Press: my project manager, Sara Cormany; my managing editor, Dori Harrell; and my copyeditor, Libby Gontarz.

Thank you to everyone who has prayed over this book and the publishing process to get this message out. Your prayers and support mean the world to me!

Grab a Cuppa

HELLO, FRIEND. I'M SO GLAD you're here! Grab a cuppa joe (or your beverage of choice), and let's talk missions!

Uh-oh, did I lose you?

No, no, I don't mean a from-the-pulpit-you-need-to-give-to-missions kind of talk. I mean a what-you-need-to-know-about-being-a-missionary-spouse kind of talk.

Has God called your family into missions?

Are you wondering if God has made the right choice?

Are you wondering what you have to offer?

Let me tell you—if God has called your husband, He has called you too. And rest assured, sister, God has made the right choice, and you have a *lot* to offer.

So, who am I, and why am I here? Well, I am a missionary spouse. I have served in Lesotho, Southern Africa, with my husband, a pilot/mechanic with Mission Aviation Fellowship (MAF), for nearly nine years. I am a stay-at-home mom, and I homeschool our two children. I was single when God called me into mission work, and I had a plan that looked exactly the opposite of what God had in store for me. I worked as a massage therapist, personal trainer, and physical therapist assistant, with an associate of applied science degree for physical therapist assistant (AAS PTA) before God called me to take my skills overseas in missions. I love my life; God has done amazing things in it. I'm just sayin' this was not my initial plan. But we'll get into plans later.

Before moving overseas, I had an opportunity to ask questions of a panel of women who had served in missions before me. But I did not know what to ask them, and sadly, they did not offer much information. They shared some funny stories and a little practical advice, like bring the right cookware, learn to cook from scratch (here's a cookbook), and burn your underwear. But they did not offer much spiritual or applicable practical advice. At the time, I didn't know that what cookware I purchased would not matter much in the long run.

I was naïve, and once I started my life overseas with my husband, I felt a bit duped. I had many unmet expectations of how my life would look. Since I was feeling ill equipped to handle some of the hardships I faced overseas, God put it on my heart to write the book I wish I'd had and use it to walk with women to prepare and equip them for their work in missions.

Maybe you are like me, and you planned to go into mission work, whether married or not. Or perhaps your calling to the mission field came with your calling to be married to a missionary. Maybe you are just exploring options after hearing a missions sermon at church. As I share some of my stories, my heart is to encourage and equip you for going into mission work with your husband no matter where you are in the journey. I want to give an honest look into preparing for missions and living life overseas and answer some of those questions I didn't know to ask. I want to share my experiences working in missions as a spouse, give simple definitions of some of the terminology, and keep things clear and concise.

I acknowledge that each person's journey overseas is different. Every woman has different experiences, even those who have gone through similar circumstances as others. And you will learn lessons through your own experience that I won't cover here. This book is not about being a better missionary, a better spouse, or a better missionary spouse. It is about bringing to light challenges that may be overlooked in missionary training. I hope to give you some tools in your toolbox to use when challenges come about. I want to send you off with more than a packing list, a cookbook, and how-to advice on disposing of your worn-out unmentionables.

I would love to sit with you over coffee and answer your questions, especially those you don't know to ask! For now, here we are. I don't have all the answers, but God has asked me to share what I've learned. I will open with my story about how God changed my call to missions. Then I will share some of the things I learned in preparing to move and some of the struggles and victories I experienced living overseas.

As I share my stories and those of other women who have walked this journey, I pray the Holy Spirit would open your heart to learn from our experiences. I pray this book helps you to feel more equipped than you would without these tools, and I hope you would refer back to this book to encourage you and remind you of your calling when challenges come. By the end, I pray you are inspired and encouraged by our stories, that you are more equipped to step into your calling, and that you may walk in confidence through your missionary adventure.

Chapter 1

Submitting to God's Plan

*As I witnessed God's beautiful composition unfold within my life,
it was as if He and I were dancing. I was like a little girl dancing
on her daddy's feet.*

AS I WALKED THROUGH THE church foyer one Sunday after service, my senior pastor pulled me aside and said, "Mari, we think you should go to Africa and marry Bryan." I stood there dumbfounded, mouth hanging open.

I finally blinked and managed to move my mouth enough to utter some semblance of speech. "Uh . . . what does he think about this?"

He looked up, cocked his head a little to one side, and said, "Well, he's not opposed to it."

Words escaped me.

Then, breaking the obviously awkward silence, he said, "Well, just pray about it," and walked away.

Woody Allen once said, "If you want to make God laugh, tell him about your plans." While many use this quote in jest, it sure fits the plot twist introduced that day in my church foyer. I was confident God had called me to long-term mission work. I was single, with a dog as my only responsibility. I had ambitious ideas. I knew where I wanted to go, with whom I wanted to work, and the work I wanted to do. And I would do it while spreading the gospel of Christ to unreached people. I was ready and willing to go. Yep, I had a plan!

My meticulously laid plans were about to get a God-sized edit.

We all have plans—until we don't—from simple scheduling to life-altering decisions. We schedule out our whole day, and one appointment gets canceled, throwing everything off. We hope to be married by twenty-five, but instead, we are having dinner with our other single friends at thirty-five. We plan to have a baby in our second year of marriage only to find ourselves at the fertility clinic after our fifth anniversary. In every facet of life, even the best-laid plans may need to change.

Think about the last time you flew on an airplane. If you haven't flown before, just dream with me. Let's make it fun and say it was for a vacation. After booking your tickets, once you were on board the airplane, you were probably so excited about your vacation that you didn't put much thought into flying. Instead, you put your complete trust in the pilot to get you where you were going.

However, there is so much more to flying than what passengers see. The flight plan, for instance. Pilots must file a flight plan with the control tower before ever getting in the cockpit. That plan not only helps the pilot to stay on course and get you to where you're going, but it also helps others keep track of the flight, just in case something happens. There are times, though, when the flight plan needs to change. The control tower will call the pilot and give him an amended flight plan. The pilot will then adapt his plan to the new one, alter the one he had laid out, and adjust his course.

Wherever you are in your missions journey, the Lord has a purpose for you. Yes, right where you are. Even when plans change, there is a purpose. Though it may not make sense at the time, it is essential to trust that God is in the control tower and respond as a pilot to an amended flight plan: adapt to the new plan, alter the one in your mind, and adjust your course. Adapt. Alter. Adjust.

Am I saying it's easy? Uh, no! I am a planner. When I travel, I am the one organizing the itinerary and printing my packing list—actually, I don't print it. I keep it on the computer in case I need to add something! If something forces me to alter my plans, I get frazzled.

I scratch and claw, clutching my plan to my chest as it's being torn from my hands. Sometimes I cling so tightly to my own agenda that I can't even see past my day planner! So no, it's not easy. But it is necessary.

Adapt, Alter, Adjust

My call to missions was not an overnight revelation. I didn't wake up one morning and decide that God was calling me to missions. It wasn't a voice from above one day telling me to drop my life and move overseas (thank you, God). No, it was a gradual call, and I had put much thought and planning into it. So this seemingly sudden potential change of direction from my pastor shook me.

I had been interested in missions for a while. One summer, I was trying to choose between a few upcoming short-term mission trips. I was very interested in joining the team going to Ukraine. Though the church canceled that trip, Ukraine held a special place in my heart. Friends in my church had traveled to Ukraine every year for twelve years. As I spent more time with them over the next year, we discussed the needs in Ukraine and possibilities for ministry. I heard of a need for someone to provide manual therapy for physically delayed and disabled children and education for their caregivers.

I was about to finish school to earn an associate's degree for physical therapist assistant (PTA). I had a background in massage therapy and exercise, and I was confident I could fill that need. A bonus was the opportunity to learn to speak Ukrainian! I love Slavic languages, and I've always wanted to learn Russian, and Ukrainian was similar. Clearly, this was a sign confirming my calling. I had no doubt; I was supposed to go to Ukraine. After graduation, I accepted an entry-level position in my new field to gain some experience. I requested the month of October off for an extended visit to Ukraine. My plans were about to come to fruition, and I was reeling with excitement.

Enter God's big red editing pen. A few months before my graduation, Dan (my mentor and the missions director at my church) had taken our senior pastor, Brandon, on a vision trip through Africa. They wanted to spend time with missionaries our church supported. One of the missionaries they visited was Bryan, a single young man who had previously attended our church. He was serving as a missionary pilot in Lesotho, a small country surrounded by South Africa.

During their lengthy commute through South Africa, Dan and Brandon decided it was up to them to find Bryan a wife. They considered the women in our church who were still single. When one of them mentioned my name, they both concurred that Bryan and I would be a perfect match. Initially, Bryan resisted the idea of being set up. So many people had tried that already. His grandmother would still tell him about her friends' single granddaughters. He thought how silly it was for his pastors to be playing matchmaker, but then again, how else was he going to find a wife while living overseas? Eventually, Dan (who had also been his mentor) encouraged him to at least write me and see where God took it. After some prayer, he agreed to write if I was open to it.

When Pastor Brandon arrived back home, I did not expect to have a conversation with him in the church foyer about who my future husband should be. My drive home that day left a vexing question tumbling through my mind: "Who is this man my pastors think I should marry?" I knew who he was, but I didn't know him. My thoughts drifted back to when we had met a few years earlier. I was preparing to go to Honduras for my first short-term mission trip, and Bryan was raising support to go overseas with MAF. He had presented his ministry at our church that morning. Pilots flying for Christ? My curiosity was piqued. I made my way to his display table, so enthusiastic about speaking with a real missionary. I just had to pick his brain. We chatted for a few minutes, I signed up for his prayer letters, and that was it. After that initial meeting, we saw each other at church occasionally, but we hardly ever talked. And then he left for Lesotho. I never thought of him in a romantic way.

Well, since Pastor Brandon had said Bryan wasn't "opposed" to the idea, I did give it some prayer. I also browsed through his photos on Facebook—don't be so shocked! I already knew he had a heart for God. I just had to find out if I thought he was cute. As I scrolled through his pictures, I felt as if I were getting to know him. It turns out I did find him very attractive, and I thought, *This might be an okay idea*. The more thought and prayer I gave this idea, the more my heart would flutter, and my mind would drift to thoughts of what could be. When Dan and I talked more about this prospective betrothal, he told me that Bryan was waiting for permission to write to me. So I gave the green light, and I waited.

Waiting on God

During that waiting period, I played the I-wonder-where-this-might-go game. My thoughts went back and forth like a tennis match. *Will he like me? Will I like him?* Time seemed to slow to a crawl. Finally, a very long month later, Bryan and I began writing to one another. After just a few messages, I knew there was a spark. My heart skipped a beat with each email notification. The first time we scheduled a video call, my pulse pounded as I paced through my living room, wringing my hands, waiting for that dancing sound of an incoming call on Skype. I fumbled to press the accept button, and I was finally able to hear his voice.

Not having the distraction of deciding what to do on a date, we had plenty of time to talk, and we were able to get to know one another extremely well and very quickly. It didn't take long before we found ourselves in a long-distance courtship. As it turns out, being set up by someone who knows both parties is not such a bad idea!

Our relationship continued to grow, and we started talking about our future—together. My heart soared at the thought of a future with Bryan, but at the same time, I was conflicted as to how this would affect my plans. As exciting as it was to think about marriage, it caused much confusion for me and my idea for missions.

Right, *my* idea for missions. Africa was not Ukraine.

It was almost as if I could hear a radio clicking with a call from God in the control tower. First, I hear the static and then the click. I adjust the frequency, and then I hear:

"Mari." . . . *click* . . . *crackling static* . . . "Mari, this is God. I have an amended flight plan for you. Stand by to copy."

"Lord?"...*click*...*static*..."Yes, Lord, standing by."...*crackling static*...

I call back....*click*..."Lord?"...*click*...*static*..."Still standing by for that amended flight plan."

Radio silence.

Something big was happening. A change was coming. I started feeling like I had been looking into a tranquil body of water, and someone threw in a boulder. I knew God was calling me to be a missionary, but I also wanted to be married. So many questions preyed on my mind, and doubts began to weigh heavy on my chest.

Night after night, I would cry out to God, "Lord, didn't you call me to Ukraine?"

"What is there for me in mission aviation?"

"Lord, is this the man you want me to marry?"

"Lord, Africa? Really? What would I do there?"

This emotional tug-of-war tore me apart by day and left me tossing in bed each night. I had been praying so long for God to bring me a godly man to share life with, and it was looking like I had finally found "the one." Would God make me choose between marriage and missions? I was so sure of where God was calling me that I actually researched to see if there were any MAF bases near Ukraine (there are not). Surely, God didn't want to send me to Africa!

During the next few months, my plans became continually muddled while God's plans were made abundantly clear. All things related to Ukraine began to fall apart. Donations that were supposed to come with us were delayed or misrouted. The administrative staff with whom my friends were connected left the ministry. Someone else filled the position I was seeking. We rescheduled the plans we had to visit multiple times, and for the second time in two years, my friends decided not to go. Finally, we canceled all our plans. The door to Ukraine was not just closed; it was slammed and locked! I couldn't even see that door anymore. There was nothing more to hold on to, but I still tried.

Complete Submission

When I started planning out my life as a missionary, I don't recall submitting my Ukraine "flight plan" to God. It was like a text message I had composed but forgot to hit send. When I look back, I can see my pride and need for control had taken over. Were the "signs" actually from God, or did I make them fit the situation? Just because I love Slavic languages, did that mean God was calling me to work in a Slavic country? I did not seek out His will. Sure, my intentions were pure—I saw a need and wanted to fill it—but I didn't take time to submit my ideas to God.

In a desperate attempt to please Him, I made my plan and asked God to bless it, saying, "Look at me, Daddy! Look what I'm going to do! Do you love me?" But instead of trusting Him, submitting to His will, and seeking to glorify Him, I tried to figure things out in my own strength, which set the stage for me to receive the glory for anything good that might have come from it instead of Him.

So, what, then? Are we to roam about this world without plans hoping God points us in the right direction? Heavens, no. Proverbs 16:9 says, "The heart of man plans his way, but the Lord establishes his steps." Yes, we should make plans and get counsel, especially the Lord's counsel, for "Without counsel plans fail, but with many advisers they succeed" (Proverbs 15:22). But also take notice of this passage from James:

> Come now, you who say, "Today or tomorrow we will go into such and such a town and spend a year there and trade and make a profit"—yet you do not know what tomorrow will bring. What is your life? For you are a mist that appears for a little time and then vanishes. Instead you ought to say, "If the Lord wills, we will live and do this or that." (James 4:13–15)

James is not telling us to roam about without plans either. Rather, he reminds us that we don't know what tomorrow brings, so he encourages us to hold on to our ideas loosely and be more attentive to God's will, even if it means changing course. So yes, make plans for what

God has put on your heart, but submit them to God and allow Him to establish your steps.

I know I heard God correctly in my call to missions. But I didn't listen to Him completely, or rather, I jumped a bit ahead of Him. In my desire to be obedient, I pounced at the first open door that made sense to me. But God doesn't always work in ways that make sense to us. During this time, the Lord gave me hope through a Bible verse that began to redirect me and help me submit entirely to God. In Proverbs 16:3, we read, "Commit your work to the Lord, and your plans will be established"

As I began to let go of my will and submit to His, I started to see God's beautiful orchestration unfold. Bryan and I were falling in love, and it appeared that marriage was just one aspect of the amended flight plan God was writing for me. So I slowly started to loosen my grip on my hopes and dreams for Ukraine, which opened my hands to receive the blessing of marriage and my new call to missions—in Africa. Though I still hoped that God might send us somewhere else, I had received a new heading. It was time to adapt, alter, and adjust.

Hold Loosely

As I began to let go of my plans for Ukraine and soften my heart toward Africa, God was able to work in my life and show me how beautiful it could be. I was able to visit Bryan in Lesotho and see the work he was doing. I met the people he worked with and those they ministered to.

When I flew with Bryan to a remote village to transport a pregnant woman to a district hospital, tears burned my eyes as I watched them load this woman into the plane. She had just traveled three hours by horseback to get to the airstrip, and now she had to be flown to another village to receive care. My body ached with hers.

I also visited a child care center—the government does not favor the term *orphanage*. I wept as the director explained that theirs was one of only a handful of centers that took in orphaned children. She went on to say all the centers lacked space, volunteers, and medical care, and all were at or above capacity, leaving many more children still on the streets. I thought my heart would explode when a group of almost ten children, all under five years old, surrounded me with outstretched arms. They were longing for touch, yearning for love, and desperate for hope.

My heart was breaking, and I'm sure God's was too. There were so many ideas and potential for ministry in Lesotho that I had not even considered. I had been self-centered, thinking I was the only one who could fill the position in Ukraine and I could not possibly serve anywhere else. The Lord was breaking down my pride and showing me how nearsighted I was being. Though I still did not have a clear direction about where I would serve, God was humbling me. I was beginning to accept this change of plan and learning to hold loosely anything that was not of the Lord.

God was also changing my heart for Him. As I witnessed His beautiful composition unfold within my life, it was as if God and I were dancing. I was like a little girl dancing on her daddy's feet. We had our own music, and we had just begun composing something new. Our relationship was no longer a one-sided conversation with me asking for His blessings and gifts. It was now a two-way conversation with me humbly on my knees saying, "Lord, help me love others like you love me, no matter where they live. Here I am, Lord . . . send me," and the Lord answering, "Go, my child."

Confirmation

During my visit, Bryan proposed! Now, I was not just accepting this new plan, but I was excited about going to Lesotho and all the possibilities that lay ahead—with my fiancé! Almost immediately after saying yes to marriage and Africa, I saw just a sliver of God's sense of humor, and I thought about that Woody Allen quote about plans and had to laugh.

When I had *finally* let go of my plans for missions in Ukraine, all those closed doors began to open back up. The administrative staff returned (we had not known it was a temporary leave), and the donations were found and made it to where they needed to be. My friends returned to Ukraine the following year and reestablished their longtime connection—without me. The position I had been seeking remained filled, making it very clear that God knew what he was doing. I was not supposed to go to Ukraine. It was all for the best—God's best.

I confided in Dan that maybe I had misheard God with my call to Ukraine. He shared with me that sometimes God entices us with an idea or vision, almost like a carrot, to get us to go in a particular direction, but then He redirects our attention to reveal something better He has for us. For example, my call to Ukraine motivated me to move in the direction I was supposed to go: toward missions. But God amended my flight plan to give me my proper heading, toward Africa.

Adapting to God's Plan

As you prepare for your missionary journey, even if you are in the middle of it, adaptability is key. Just like flight plans, life plans can change. Some changes happen quickly, maybe overnight. Others happen more slowly, even over a few years. They can change a little, like a slight deviation, or a lot, turning your world upside down. Changes range from minor inconveniences—such as delayed or canceled flights, or lost luggage—to a bit more significant—a delayed departure because you need to raise more support or need more training for your organization. Then again, it could be God-sized changes, like receiving a different calling in the middle of preparing for what you thought would be your new life overseas! Plans are good, but it's necessary to hold our plans loosely so that if—dare I say *when*—things change, it will be easier to say yes to God.

As you ponder the story of how God changed my direction and how I learned to adapt, alter, and adjust, take a moment to assess the plans you have laid out. Perhaps you are like me, with a clear direction you plan to go, and something has happened to indicate that a change may be developing. Maybe you are just feeling out this idea of missions, and you want to know what you might be getting yourself into. Perhaps you are in the middle of your journey, and you wonder, *Is this all there is or what's next?* It could even be that you plan to stay put, but you picked up this book because you hear that still, small voice suggesting there may be more.

Throughout our lives as followers of Christ, we have to be just that—followers—and allow Him to lead us rather than trying to get Him to follow our plans. Wherever we find ourselves in our missionary journey, *submitting* to God and *following* Him each day are crucial to that journey. We need to stay in tune with God and be sure of His direction. We need to be adaptable and choose to listen to God's voice despite how it may sound to us or those around us. When He gives a direction, we need to move forward in faith. And if He redirects, we need to adapt, alter, and adjust our heading bearing true north, His north. Then watch the grandiosity of His handiwork unfold!

Reflection:
Think of the words *adapt*, *alter*, and *adjust*.
- What feelings rise up in your heart with these terms?
- What would you say you typically do when God edits your plans?

Think about what it means to be completely submitted to God.
- What things do you still need to submit to God?
- On what plans do you need to loosen your grip?

Think about the direction God is leading you.
- What needs to change in order to follow God, bearing true north—His north?
- What steps do you need to take to implement that change?

Take your plans and ideas to God and ask Him for direction and guidance.

If you have people in your life who are praying for you, ask them to come alongside you and pray for discernment.

I invite you to pray with me.

Prayer:
Father God, I implore the Holy Spirit to intercede on my behalf. I have tried to take control and force my own plans into fruition. You know

the desires of my heart. I pray my heart would be properly aligned with yours. Please give me clarity and help me discern your plans, and adjust my plans as needed. In Jesus's name, I pray, amen.

CHAPTER 2

Finding Identity in Christ

The world doesn't give us our identity. Who we are is based on whose we are, and we belong to Jesus.

WITH A LOOK OF DETERMINATION on her face and sweat beading on her forehead, she gritted her teeth. Her arms trembled as she pulled herself up in the parallel bars. As she steadied herself, she caught her breath. Her furrowed brow relaxed, and her eyes disappeared as her mouth turned upward in a celebratory grin. My patient stood on her own for the first time in two months. My countenance shifted from therapist to friend. My face lit up as I shouted and cheered to celebrate this monumental success. She had put in all the hard work, but being part of that moment as her physical therapist gave me a great sense of honor. We were a team. I was using my God-given gifts to affect the lives and well-being of others while serving God.

A few months later, I was the patient. As I sat in the waiting room at my doctor's office, tears filled my eyes as I pondered my caseload for the next week. *Could I still do a little?* Pain seared through my spine, jolting me back to reality. I cursed my body for its betrayal. I thought of my patients who were almost ready to be discharged, just a visit or two away from their own celebrations. One had only one more strength test to work through. I leaned forward, trying to get more comfortable, and put my elbows on my knees and my face in my hands. My shoulders shook with my sobs as I thought about another therapist taking over my caseload. *Who am I if I cannot do what God has gifted me to do?*

I was grappling with pain that prevented me from doing a job that I loved and gave me so much of my identity. This situation made me take an honest look at how I identified myself. Chances are, as you step out in obedience to God's calling on your life, you will find yourself in situations that shake you and cause you to examine how you define yourself. One question to ask yourself and get firmly grounded in before you move overseas is, Where do you find your identity?

There are many opportunities for ministry overseas. Maybe you are planning to work with orphaned children or to counsel women who have experienced crises. Perhaps you are hoping to plant a church or establish a women's ministry. Or maybe you plan to stay at home and minister to your family and possibly even homeschool your children. All of these are admirable goals. However, that is not where your identity is. If God were to present a different opportunity for ministry, after praying and discerning His direction, it would be necessary to adapt, alter, and adjust to the role He has truly called you to.

Struggling with Uncertainty

Bryan had returned to America just before I was injured. Unfortunately, after a month of treatment, it was apparent I would not be returning to work. As we sat at my dining room table poring over our budget, seeing the numbers on the screen made my face flush. I found myself questioning if Bryan would genuinely want to marry me. Being injured was enough of a burden; now my school and auto loans (and now medical bills) would be ours. I shuddered at the absurdity of the meager earnings I had to contribute. My mind and emotions taunted me. Tears stung my eyes as I looked pleadingly at Bryan. I did not picture going into a marriage disabled and unemployed.

In his quiet, gentle nature, Bryan tenderly lifted my chin to look me in the eyes. I could see the kindness on his face through my tears. He wrapped me in his strong arms and assured me that everything would be fine. I could almost feel his mischievous grin, and he chuckled a little. He reminded me that I would have had to quit my job to join MAF in just a few months anyway. I snickered, but the tears continued to fall as I buried my head in his chest.

Resting in the knowledge that Bryan loved me reminded me that God loved me too. So I clung to Proverbs 3:5–6: "Trust in the Lord with all your heart, and do not lean on your own understanding. In all your ways acknowledge him, and he will make straight your paths." And I tried to put my trust in God and what He was doing in our lives.

Getting married was a significant life change for both of us, of course. Still, it affected Bryan and me quite differently. Marrying Bryan and moving to Africa was turning my plans upside down. I was leaving the security of America and my family, friends, and church. I was heading on an unknown adventure not knowing what God had for me, especially now that I wouldn't be able to work as a PTA.

On the other hand, it seemed to me, Bryan was simply gaining a wife and going back to work as usual. He knew the job he was doing, the people he was working with, and what was expected of him. He also knew that being away was putting a burden on his team. As we shared our morning prayers, Bryan would pray that God would quickly get us back to Africa. I would quietly pray that we might have a bit more time. As I struggled with the unknown, he was struggling with the wait. While I was okay getting my feet wet slowly, he was eager to return to do the work God called him to do.

As part of an aviation organization, Bryan's job was obvious: pilot/mechanic. When we would share about our ministry, the most frequently asked question directed to me was, "What are you going to do over there?" My thoughts would drift back to the plans I had laid to rest and the confidence I once had in them. I knew they asked this question out of genuine love and curiosity, so I would fight back my tears, swallow the lump in my throat, and answer the best I could.

Raising that question was not an attempt to make me feel inadequate. It is just a product of our American culture. In our society, the most common question asked when people meet others is "What do you do for a living?" Have you ever asked or been asked this seemingly innocent question? We mean well, right? It's just a conversation starter, an icebreaker. It is even asked of children in the future tense starting as early as five or six years old: "What do you want to do when you grow up?" Did you have an answer to that at six years old? Or are you like me and still didn't know well into your twenties? What of those who don't have or want a typical job to earn a living? How many of us would change that icebreaker question to ask, "Who are you?" Or better yet, "Whose are you?"

Okay, this is not a chapter on changing the narrative of intro-ductory conversations in our American culture. I just wanted to point out that it is ingrained in our history that each person contributes to society somehow. How we do that has become somewhat of an identity marker. Some family names are even given based on trades histori-cally done by that family. For example, the common name Smith, the name of a man who worked with metal, means "to smite or strike." My maiden name, Morgan, a name used for sailors, means "sea defender" or "sea captain." My married name, Eygabroad, is a combination of a poulterer and a baker, "eggs" and "bread." Contributing to society and making a living are great things. But is what we do for a living truly where our identity lies?

Staying with the Baggage
One Sunday during a presentation, I shared about the many ministry options revealed during my visit to Africa and that I just didn't know what God had in store. I tried to stay poised, optimistic, and confident, but my insecurities betrayed me. When we finished our presentation, tears began to well in my eyes. I quickly excused myself to regain my composure. That question was asked so often, I felt I needed to have an answer.

When I returned to the church auditorium, Bryan spoke with a slightly older woman, who had asked if she could talk with both of us. I noticed her friendly face as she took my hands gently in hers and introduced herself. Her soft eyes met mine. Letting out a gentle sigh, she softly patted my hand. She invited us both to sit as she shared a new interpretation of a story from 1 Samuel 30. I invite you to find this story in your Bible, but I will paraphrase it here:

> David and his men had come to Ziklag. They discovered that the Amalekites had made a raid against the Negev and against Ziklag and had taken captive wives, sons, and daughters. David's two wives were among those captured. David was distressed; the people wanted to stone him! But he strengthened himself in the Lord and then inquired of the Lord if he should go after the band that had raided. The Lord told him to pursue, and he would overcome.
>
> So David set out with six hundred men. They reached a brook, and two hundred men were too exhausted to cross, so they stayed behind, and David pursued with four hundred men. They came upon the Amalekites, and David struck them down, recovering what had been taken. They rescued all who were taken captive and all the flocks and herds.
>
> When David returned to the two hundred men who had stayed behind, he greeted them. Some men did not want to share the spoils with those who had stayed behind. David told them, "You shall not do so, my brothers, with what the Lord has given us. He has preserved us and given into our hand the band that came against us. Who will listen to you in this matter? For as his share is who goes down into the battle, so shall his share be who stays by the baggage. They shall share alike" (vv. 23–24). And he made it a rule for Israel from that day forward (1 Samuel 30:1–25, my paraphrase).

With our hands still folded together, my gaze remained fixed on hers as she shared. She did not focus on the God-ordained victory of King David but on those who had stayed by the brook. David declared those who remained with the baggage would receive an equal share in the spoils. Though they had stayed behind, their role for that battle was not a lesser one and did not make them any less a part of David's army.

Her story took an unexpected turn as she shared about her time on the mission field as a wife and mother. Her tears threatened to fall as she shared memories about the sweet times and the struggles of raising a family on the mission field. Like me, she had struggled with whether or not she was doing enough for the kingdom of God, sometimes feeling as if she were just "staying with the baggage." But she discovered that supporting her husband and raising their children as disciples of Christ was her most fulfilling ministry.

No Role Is Inferior

My tears splashed down on our still-joined hands. God had clearly sent this woman with a message aimed directly at my heart. In attempting to find my identity in my work, I dismissed the role of a wife and mom as somehow lesser. I wanted to be a wife and a mom. I even dreamed of staying at home. Despite that, I still believed that to be considered "in ministry," I must have a role outside the home. I was focused on what job I could do for God using my gifts and talents. I was more concerned with "the glory that comes from man than the glory that comes from God" (John 12:43).

As my new friend was sharing, her story allowed me to see the depth of another Bible passage. You may be very familiar with it, but let's take a look at 1 Corinthians:

> For the body does not consist of one member but of many. If the foot should say, "Because I am not a hand, I do not belong to the body," that would not make it any less a part of the body. And if the ear should say, "Because I am not an eye, I do not belong to the body," that would not make it any less a part of the body. If the whole body were an eye, where would be the sense of hearing? If the whole body were an ear, where would be the sense of smell? But as it is, God arranged the members in the body, each one of them, as he chose. If all were a single member, where would the body be? As it is, there are many parts, yet one body (1 Corinthians 12:14–20).

These verses tell us that everyone has a role in the kingdom of God. If God were to call me to raise a family, I would be the only one

He would want to do that job. He wouldn't want anyone else to do it for me. This woman opened my mind to even more possibilities by sharing this story. I started to see that ministry at home would not be a lesser role, and it is even okay for me to want that to be my calling. Even so, one reality was still not sinking in: my identity is not found in what I do.

Beautifully Broken

When my injury prevented me from working full time in physical therapy any longer, I felt I had lost my identity. I believed that if I didn't know what I was going to do, I didn't know who I was. I found it difficult to wrap my mind around the idea that our identity is found in Christ and what He did for us on the cross. I couldn't figure out what that looked like. How could it be that it has nothing to do with what we do? Paul said it in a way that helped me begin to understand: "Set your minds on things that are above, not on things that are on the earth. For you have died, and your life is hidden with Christ in God" (Colossians 3:2–3). It's not about our job, spouse, ministry, or our children, but about where our heart is focused.

When I accepted Jesus as my Savior, part of me felt like a fraud, believing I was too broken to be used by God. I thought I was "used goods" beyond redemption. Sure, I knew I was forgiven, and my life with Christ would be different, but I was certain God couldn't use me for anything. Maybe that's why I felt I had to *do* something to earn my salvation. I am sure it was part of God's divine plan that I could no longer do the work I wanted to do. It was a painful reminder that salvation is not something we can earn.

God reminded me that it was my brokenness that brought me to Him. He showed me that I could minister to people just by being myself and allowing Him to work in and through me. When I share what God has done in my life, it enables others to see God. When I allow people to see that I don't have my life together and that I still make mistakes—even in my walk with Christ—it gives people a sense of freedom to approach not just me but also God.

We need not be ashamed of the circumstances that brought us to Christ. Think about when you have heard a powerful testimony of someone's life being transformed by the love of Christ. Does it make you think less of them or more of God? I have a tattoo on my ankle that is covering another tattoo. I was nervous about wearing shorts for a long time for fear someone would see my tattoo and think less of me. But the tattoo underneath is a reminder of the part of my life that broke me; the tattoo that covers it is a reminder of the One who saved me. I no longer hide my tattoo because if someone does notice and ask about it, that is an open door to share about the redeeming power of Jesus Christ.

Being open and vulnerable, without trying to hide our insecurities and doubts, is not a sign of weakness but of authenticity. If others see it as a weakness, well, we can take comfort in the words of the apostle Paul:

> [The Lord] said to me, "My grace is sufficient for you, for *my power is made perfect in weakness.*" Therefore *I will boast . . . of my weaknesses*, so that the power of Christ may rest upon me. For the sake of Christ, then, I am content with weaknesses, insults, hardships, persecutions, and calamities. For *when I am weak, then I am strong.* (2 Corinthians 12:9–10)

Orbiting Around Jesus

A friend of mine gave me an excellent analogy of what it means to have our identity in Christ. Think of identity in terms of the solar system. In our solar system, all the planets move on their orbits revolving around the sun. There is order when all the planets are revolving in their own orbit. If the sun were to go away, there would be chaos. All the planets would spin out of control and crash into one another, and the solar system would cease to exist. Planets also have moons, but the moons revolve around the planet, not vice versa.

People are like planets; Jesus is like the sun. Each of our lives revolves around Jesus in its own orbit. We also have things orbiting in our lives like moons—spouses, children, work, etc. These "moons" are good things unless our lives begin to revolve around them. For example, let's say I have two moons: a spouse and a child. If I have another child, I gain another moon, and it starts orbiting in my life. I must make adjustments, but it shouldn't change my orbit around Jesus. If one of my moons were to fall away, it would cause a void and likely a lot of pain, but I would not spin out of control as a planet, because my orbit is still around the Son.

I had focused on what I wanted to do, a moon, rather than on whom I was doing it for, the Son. If I had kept my focus on Jesus, I would still feel the pain of letting go of my plans and my job, but it would not have been such a devastating loss. I would not feel as if I'd lost my identity.

Maybe you are taking a look at your moons and starting to see bits of your life controlled by things other than Christ. Sometimes, even the good things we take on can distract us from Christ. When you look at your work, ministry, family schedules, or other commitments that occupy your time, heart, or thoughts, do you see Christ at the center?

Lavished with God's Love

In his letters, Paul the apostle identifies himself as a slave, a bondservant, or an apostle of Christ. He does not talk about the job that he does, the family he came from, or boast in his ministry; not as part of his identity anyway. When he speaks of his heritage or past (Philippians 3:5 and Acts 22:3), it is to bring clarity to who he had been and who he was becoming. Paul has set aside his former way of life and now simply identifies himself as a servant of God, and his only focus is sharing the gospel of Christ.

We don't work to gain favor or prove our faith. The work we do comes from the love that God pours into us. John says, "See what great love the Father has *lavished* on us, that we should be called children of God!" (1 John 3:1 NIV). God *lavishes* his love on us. To lavish means to bestow something in generous or extravagant quantities. God is so gracious with His love that it overflows, so much that we can't help but do good works. Whether we have an outside ministry or our ministry is in the home, God's love flows through us in all things. We do work out of a passion for God and because of God's love toward us. Our works pour *out* of us as a love offering because of the love God pours *into* us.

The story that woman shared of David came at a time when my heart was torn in many directions. Her message allowed my mind to climb out of the box it was trapped in and imagine what it could be like to truly live for Christ no matter what I was doing. If God were to call me to be a stay-at-home wife and mom, I could do that job to the best of my ability for God, and He would honor that. If I chose to find a ministry outside the home, He would honor that as well, and I could be at peace knowing I am a child of God; that is where my identity is. It is not in what I do.

Maybe you are finding yourself in a similar situation. Perhaps you find yourself having to let go of your dreams and go in a new direction. Maybe you have been searching for identity in what you do or who you married or in your plans. Perhaps your life seems like it's about to spin out of control. It may be time to shift focus. Turn your eyes upon Jesus. Remember, "Whatever you do, work heartily, *as for the Lord and not for men*, knowing that from the Lord you will receive the inheritance as your reward. You are serving the Lord Christ" (Colossians 3:23–24). Anything you choose to do, if you do it as unto the Lord, out of pure love for Him, and allow His love to flow through you, He will honor it.

Reflection:

Think about all the roles you fill in your life.

- Which of your roles gives you a sense of identity?
- Of all the roles God could choose for you, which ones do you think feel lesser?

Think about your "moons," the things revolving in your life—spouse, kids, job, etc.

- Which of your "moons" might hold more gravitational pull than Jesus in your life?

- What needs to happen to shift your focus back to Jesus?
- What would happen if one of your "moons" were to go away?

Think about the things you *do* to gain acceptance or *earn* love.

- How does it make you feel to know that God lavishes His love on you to overflow in your life?
- What would it look like if you were to work because of God's love, rather than to earn His love?

Take a moment to reflect on Colossians 3:2–3; "Set your minds on things that are above, not on things that are on the earth. For you have died, and your life is hidden with Christ in God" How can this verse transform how you find your identity in Christ?

I invite you to pray with me.

Prayer:

Father God, I confess I have sought my identity in worldly things. I pray you would help me see who you have created me to be. Help me tear down my idols. Help me put the things of my life in their proper place and keep you at the center. Help me keep my focus on you and see where my identity is found. In Jesus's name, I pray, amen.

CHAPTER 3

Information and Expectations

Disappointment is typically a result of unmet expectations.

ROLLED OVER AND LOOKED AT the clock. My heart jumped, and I shot out of bed and darted to the closet. I grabbed the nearest outfit and threw it on. I was already breaking a sweat. I quickly brushed my teeth and tied my hair up in a messy bun. *No time for makeup*, I thought. I grabbed my socks and shoes, and I hustled downstairs. I dropped my footwear by the door and hurried into the kitchen to grab some coffee and toast to go. I caught a glimpse of Bryan out of the corner of my eye. "What happened to the alarm? Why didn't you wake me up?" I huffed as I fumbled in the cabinet for a coffee mug.

The stillness in the kitchen made me pause. Holding an empty mug, I glanced toward the dining room table to see Bryan looking up at me, his eyebrows raised, eyes wide, and his coffee cup halfway to his face. His laptop was open, and when I made eye contact, he gave a slight head nod to the seat next to his to reveal a second cup of coffee on the table. My face flushed, and my shoulders slumped. I returned the mug to the cabinet as I gave Bryan an apologetic grin. I shuffled my feet as I went to give him a good-morning kiss and plopped into the chair next to his. I wrapped my hands around my coffee cup and brought it to my face. I breathed in the aroma of fresh coffee and exhaled a sigh of relief. I would not be late for work; I was already there. And so was Bryan. "Sorry, babe. Good morning. Thank you for the coffee."

Working Together from Home

If you haven't heard the term yet, *deputation* is the time missionaries spend raising support in preparation for going to the mission field. Most people will stop working their full-time job to put all their time and effort into raising prayer and financial support. Our first year of marriage and deputation started at about the same time. Since Bryan is a pilot, let me use some pilot lingo. Bryan and I were now pilot and copilot. We were paired up in a cramped cockpit, trying to figure out how to work, live, and be together all day, every day without the luxury of a handbook. Each of us had been flying solo most of our lives. Now we were fumbling to figure out where to sit, which controls were ours, and who was in control of takeoffs and landings!

I am certainly not complaining! It was a gift to have that first year at home together as newlyweds, but that also meant we saw the best and worst of each other. There was no putting on a facade. Neither of us was leaving the house for work. Tempers flew, funny noises emerged, barriers were broken. Our first year was a year of grace. We must offer grace to have healthy relationships with anyone, romantic or otherwise. One definition of grace is *undeserved* favor upon someone. When I huffed into the kitchen that morning with my little messy bun, I needed grace. Bryan allowed me to be myself without judgment. He poured out his grace on me. He also learned that we probably shouldn't interact much until I have had coffee.

Prior to your journey into missions, you and your spouse have likely been apart during the day. Either one or both of you worked. Perhaps there has even been some training for missions outside of work hours, keeping the two of you separated for most of the day. Before you begin working at home together, there should be an ongoing conversation about expectations. It is essential to offer grace to one another and clarify what needs to be done each day and divide the tasks so you each has a role to fill. Who will be doing phone calls? Who will be doing emails? Who will be writing thank-you cards? Establishing an agreed-upon quitting time is also essential, as you want to protect your downtime.

As Bryan and I learned about one another and learned to communicate, we began to work well together. Our expectations of one another became clearer, and things started to work a lot smoother. Each day we would list what needed to be done, and together we decided who would be doing what. For instance, I hate talking on the phone. Seriously, I don't even like to order pizza. So phone calls were on Bryan's task list because during deputation, phone calls have to be made. When you have a clear picture of what each of you is responsible for, it makes for a better working environment.

While Bryan is the one in charge of phone calls, I am on the computer. Any research or writing that needs to be done, I'm your girl. One thing Bryan teases me about is tabs. I usually have many tabs open in my internet browser. At the time of this writing, I have thirty-nine tabs open! Okay, this could be considered digital hoarding, and I may need help. But I like those tabs! If I need that information later, I don't want to search for it again. With a quick glance, I can see what web page it is, and it's easily accessible with the tap of a finger. There is no way I could store all that information in my head. But there is such a thing as information overload, even for information junkies!

Before I move on, I would like to clarify some more terms. You may be familiar with them, but in case you're not, let's cover them here. I'll start with *candidacy*. This is the process an organization uses to select missionaries who fit its model for missionary service. *Security training* teaches missionaries how to be safe, especially in a foreign culture. *Ministry partnership training* teaches those selected missionaries how to raise support during their deputation process, which I defined earlier.

Information Overload

Bryan and I spent five weeks at MAF headquarters as we went through candidacy. Then through security training, followed by ministry partnership training. And with that, we were on our own for deputation. On our last day at headquarters, Bryan and I were given a box full of material for deputation, including our prayer cards, business cards, and other items for ministry promotion. Everything was mysteriously wrapped in brown paper so we would not inadvertently see the new MAF logo to be released the following week. We resisted the temptation to peek early.

When the time came to open it, we sat in our dining room and tore into that box like kids with a Christmas package. As we ripped through that brown paper, it was like a flood of information all over again. So, there we were. I had a ton of information. Unlike the tabs in my browser, this was all in my brain, and none of it was marked. It was like an information highway without a map. It was time to organize our brains, our promotion material, and our schedule and start deputation!

Bryan and I would spend the week before a church presentation preparing for our visit. If we were sharing at a church that supported Bryan when he was single, Bryan would spend time preparing me. He would tell me about some people I might meet during our visit, how they met, and how they came to begin supporting his (now our) ministry. His heart for these friends was apparent, and I could see he genuinely loved each one. I had a heavy feeling in my chest thinking of the connections Bryan had with so many people and that now I would have those connections as well. I didn't have many relationships, so adding so many at one time was a bit overwhelming. And we were preparing to meet even more people and visit even more churches.

Deputation can be a stressful time. The pressure of building a support team, sometimes with a deadline looming, can feel intimidating. I tend to get nervous connecting with churches and individuals, so managing anxiety is another challenge. My mind buzzed as I tried to remember all we learned in training in addition to the relationships I was learning about. But God started working in my heart, reminding me that it is not just about sharing the information but building relationships.

Others' Unmet Expectations
Deputation often includes a lot of travel. Though Bryan and I travel quite a bit, I think we probably travel the least of the missionaries in

our organization. About a month after completing our training, we began a four-week road trip down the West Coast, the goal being speaking at churches and meeting with supporters.

This trip would include staying with family, friends, and even people we hadn't met. It would be just the two of us, a few months married, and my troublemaker husky, Austin, who had been my companion for the previous nine years. This trip was sure to keep us on our toes and out of our comfort zone. We would be living out of suitcases, sleeping in a different bed every few days, and sharing space with others—not to mention the countless hours of driving.

Out of the gate, we planned to stay with Bryan's family for a week. Being newly married, sharing our personal space with one another was already stretching us. Now we were daring to share space with our family? Bryan assured me we would be fine. We were staying for one week. I could do anything for a week.

During this particular family stay, we would take our computers to a coffee shop in town, which would allow us to work uninterrupted and avoid listening to the news all day. Working at the coffee shop also allowed us to schedule short coffee visits with friends and work between appointments. That week was also pretty packed with dinner engagements.

We visited with our family over breakfast and in the afternoons when we finished with our workday. After a few days, we noticed some tension in the house. When we asked about it, we discovered they were expecting us to have dinner with them each evening. We thought they understood that we were working and not just there for a visit. As we discussed the issue, we made arrangements to have dinner with them for the next two nights. That seemed to smooth things out. As we pondered the situation, we realized it was not so much about us visiting with them but a matter of unmet expectations.

Disappointment is typically a result of unmet expectations. If you have ever disappointed someone, you know it probably was not anything in particular you did, but that they had unmet expecta- tions of you. When you call upon family or friends for hospitality, it is essential to ask what they expect during your time with them. Would they like you to join them for dinner every night? Perhaps a printout of your schedule would help clarify your appointments and obligations, so they know what they can expect and when. If we had given our family a plan, perhaps they would have offered more grace for not joining them for dinner.

Let Them Be Jesus

One of our next stops found us in the home of someone we had not met, which is not uncommon when visiting churches. Our host, Beth, was a member of one of our supporting churches who had the gift of hospitality. She opened her home to us as she would to her own family. As we pulled into her drive, she greeted us with hugs and Austin with pup treats. She showed us around her home, and her face lit up as she introduced us to her children and grandchildren through the pictures that lined the walls.

I could feel Jesus in her home and her heart. She showed us to the kitchen and encouraged us to make ourselves at home. Then she showed us to our room and gave us time to unpack and settle in as she gave Austin a more thorough tour of her home and showed him the all-important doggy door. Unlimited access to the outdoors! Our boy was beside himself with joy as he ran around exploring the yard and getting to know her little dog.

Like Beth, those who offer to host missionaries typically attend the churches we visit. They understand we are there to work, and sometimes they would even have our schedule from the church. There are usually little to no expectations for visiting. We learned that it is good to schedule visits with host families as we (now) would for our own family. It is a way to be courteous, express gratitude, and get to know our hosts.

Beth did have our schedule. The mission committee at the church scheduled most of our speaking engagements and appointments for us, like a community service project we helped with; we just had to show up on time. While this took some pressure off us, it also left us feeling somewhat out of our element. We were accustomed to filling our schedule, but now almost everything was laid out for us. The lack of control of our plans felt awkward at times, but we could roll with it.

Maybe you are someone who might shy away from being put up by strangers. If so, pray and ask God to work in your heart. In many ways, it is easier to stay in a stranger's home. For instance, Beth had a God-given gift of hospitality, and it is important to allow others to work in their spiritual gifts. As it says in Hebrews, "Do not neglect to show hospitality to strangers, for thereby some have entertained angels unawares" (Hebrews 13:2).

Of all the places we visited, that week of staying with someone we did not know and having the church tell us where to go and when proved to be the least stressful week of our road trip. Bryan and I (and Austin) felt so at home at Beth's house that we found it difficult to leave. Her hospitality put us at ease from the very beginning. She welcomed us into her home, troublemaker dog and all, without expectation. This unconditional love from a stranger was like Jesus with skin on.

Our Own Unmet Expectations
After three weeks of a full schedule, we were ready for some downtime. So for the final leg of our road trip, we enjoyed a week of "we time." There were no appointments or church visits scheduled during that time, so we decided to take a scenic route home. It was a beautiful drive, and we took our time. We stopped at viewpoints, walked trails in the forests, and had picnics on a few beaches.

For our next overnight stay, I had reserved what I thought was a wonderful waterfront inn with a sunset view. During our drive, we talked about relaxing and enjoying a peaceful sunset. We were looking forward to this respite. After ten hours of driving, we arrived at the hotel. I looked up at the sign as Bryan parked the car. I tilted my head to try to get a better look. I looked at the GPS and pulled out my reservation to double-check the name and address. I turned to Bryan. "Where are we? This can't be right." I handed the paper to Bryan, and we both rechecked the address. We were in the right place, all right; it was just nothing like what I thought I had booked.

This "inn" was straight out of a horror movie. A small two-story motel with old faded blue paint on the outside and the baked-in smell of cigarette smoke on the inside. On the bed were what looked like thirty-year-old linens, and next to the bed were two old wooden tables with ashtrays and cigarette burns. The "sunset view" was across a vast parking lot, watching the sun dip down behind the massive supermarket. We enjoyed the "waterfront" view of swampland that lay about twelve feet outside the back door of our room, across a small patch of soggy grass. It was too late to cancel or find anything else, so we settled in as best we could. We were staying for one night; we could do anything for one night.

Perhaps you have reserved hotels online before, and you have a mixed bag of experiences. Online booking is great, but sometimes you don't get what you expect. My takeaway for booking online is to keep your hopes high and your expectations low. It is a challenge to find hotels that allow pets, but this one . . . this one takes the cake for the worst decision ever. (I have since challenged that title, but that's a story for another day.)

Despite our bewilderment, we were thankful we had a place to lay our heads that night. On the upside, since we were right next to a supermarket, we stopped in to grab something for dinner. We also grabbed some snacks and other essentials for our drive the next day, saving us a stop on the way out of town.

Traveling can be a great learning experience. Our road trip was an excellent opportunity for Bryan and me to get to know one another even better. In just four short weeks, we witnessed how each of us responds to unexpected events, plans changing, submitting to the plans of others, living out of suitcases, and unmet expectations. Since the beginning of our relationship, we had been getting to know one another quickly, and it seemed that was not changing soon. We were finally getting a feel for this cockpit we were sharing and which controls were ours. The coming months would stretch us even further as we continued in our deputation.

Now that you are a little more familiar with what deputation is, let me tell you what deputation is not. Some people believe that since we (missionaries) have left our full-time jobs, this is time off. Let's clear this up here: Deputation is not vacation. Deputation is work! Each mission organization expects its candidates to be putting in at least forty hours a week during deputation. Most put in more! That includes traveling, presentations, dinners, phone calls, emails, etc.

So when your girlfriend asks you how your vacation is going, you may want to gently remind her that you are working a forty-plus-hour work week. You must be able to differentiate between what deputation is and is not. Communicating clearly, establishing expectations, traveling long distances, and visiting people are all part of deputation, but they are not the whole picture.

Greater Expectations

One missionary spouse, Rachel, confessed that the most significant thing she is learning as a new missionary is how to deal with her own unmet expectations of how she thought missionary life was supposed to look. It's one thing to clarify expectations of friends and family members, but what about our organization and missionaries within it? For example, why do those in the organization handle finances and member care the way they do? And why are other missionaries behaving the way they are? And why do the nationals in her host country do things one way when it would be much easier to do it differently?

Rachel is smart to remind herself that if she lets these unmet expectations simmer, they will grow into resentment and bitterness. She says,

> As a follower of Christ, I have to remind myself regularly I am expected to glorify Christ. That's it . . . I can't expect the organization or coworkers to act a certain way. That is between them and God. If I put all my trust in an organization, I will always be disappointed. The organization is not Jesus. They cannot handle the pressure of being a perfect

Savior. Our only hope is to put all our trust in Jesus, who has restored our relationship with God. We can bring our needs before God, just like a loving Father. We can trust Him and have perfect peace about doing what He wills. You can rely on Him. He will not disappoint you. (R. Welge, personal communication, June 12, 2021)

My friend is not alone in her lament. Many missionaries have left the mission field or an organization because they disagreed with leadership. It is important to remember that organizations are businesses. Though our business is to be about God's business, if you want a salary, organizations have to make money. And organizations are run by people. People are imperfect. If you have a question about how or why something is done, rather than telling them something needs to change, it would be prudent to approach leadership in a position of humility and ask. If their answer is along the lines of "That's just the way it's always been done," maybe you could prod a little more and see if there may be a better way.

Seek to Understand

Perhaps you see some areas in which you feel your organization or the people within it could improve. My prayer is that you would not let what you consider inefficiency overshadow the overarching goal of sharing the gospel. We should be slow to anger, correct, or speak and quick to give grace, pray, and listen. Above all, we should seek to honor God in all our ways, "for the anger of man does not produce the righteousness of God" (James 1:20). Allowing our frustration over the practices of an organization or a culture to rise in our hearts only feeds bitterness and undermines our effectiveness in ministry. If the fruit of the ministry honors God, unless the methods are outright against moral ethics or illegal, is it worth the effort to press for change for the sake of efficiency?

As we join an organization or a team on the field, we must seek to understand the "whys" of those before us before coming in guns blazing with how things need to change. Asking questions is fine, but if we watch and observe for a time, we may discover that how they are doing things is best. Also, when working in a non-Western culture, the Western way is not necessarily the best way. If a change does need to happen, we should think of change in an organization like turning a big ship.. The bigger the ship (organization), the slower the turn (change), but even a small rudder can turn a large ship. We also need to be willing to step up and be the change we seek. If we are not ready to help implement the change, there is little motivation for leadership to do it for us.

Much like we can't understand God's ways, we often won't understand the ways of our spouse, our family, our friends, or our organization. In his book *The Seven Habits of Highly Effective People*, Dr. Stephen Covey says, "Seek first to understand, then to be understood." If we couple that with a verse from Proverbs 1:6, "Let the wise hear and increase in learning, and the one who understands obtain guidance," we can get a bigger picture that shows us it is wise to seek to learn and understand what we are facing, and wiser still to obtain guidance.

I will discuss the support-raising aspects of deputation in more detail in the next chapter, but all the planning, organizing, connecting, and juggling information we receive during this time can be overwhelming. It is imperative to realize that we all have expectations whether we communicate them or not. When we have a lot on our plate, we tend to overlook things. We may not even know we have expectations until they go unmet. When we have a situation that causes friction in our hearts, it would be wise to take a closer look to determine whether this is an expectation that is going unmet. Knowing how to tell when that is the case will serve you well for deputation and your time on the field.

Reflection:
Think about what it will be like to work with your spouse from home.
- What are some things you and your spouse can discuss to clarify expectations before working together?

- What tasks do you see that need to get done? Which of those fit your gifts, and which of them fit with your spouse?

Think about what it means to be on deputation.

- How would you describe or define deputation to those who ask?
- What expectations do you have when staying with others?
- How would you determine your host's expectations before staying in their home?

Think about how you respond when your expectations go unmet.

- How will you adapt, alter, and adjust when things don't measure up to your expectations?
- If changes do need to be made, how can you address them in humility, and what can you do to help implement them?

I invite you to pray with me.

Prayer:

Father God, I pray for your guidance as my husband and I figure out how to work together. I pray you would help us figure out where to sit in this cockpit and show us which controls we are responsible for. I pray we may pour out grace on one another and lift one another up in prayer as we venture into what is new territory for both of us. I pray for your grace for the challenges of staying with family or friends, and for your intercession as we clarify expectations of us. I also pray for discernment in explaining what deputation is to those who may not understand. Help us to understand what we expect of others, our organization, and our team. In Jesus's name, I pray, amen.

Chapter 4

Support Raising

*God has called some people to go, and He has called
others to send.*

MY FINGERS REFUSED TO MOVE as I sat at my computer, trying to find the words to put in an email. This task paralyzed me, and it wasn't even a phone call. The idea of writing to someone to ask for money intimidated me. The very thought of this deputation concept was daunting. When Bryan and I went through candidacy, Bryan was getting a refresher course, but to me, everything was brand new. I was so thankful that he had done this before! The only experience I had with raising support was when I had gone on short-term mission trips. Even then, when I was preparing for my first trip, I tried to figure out how I could come up with the money myself. I wondered, *Who am I that others would want to give money to send me on a mission trip?*

During that time, someone told me that by not offering others the opportunity to be a part of my ministry, I robbed them of the chance to be a blessing. The Lord did incredible work in my heart through that, reminding me that He has called some people to go, and He has called others to send. Most people want to bless others with the gifts God has given them, be it a financial contribution, a material donation, or just giving of their time or gifts of hospitality. They just need or want to be presented with an opportunity.

When Bryan and I started our deputation process, while I still felt awkward about asking others for support, that lesson echoed in my mind. I certainly didn't want to rob others of a chance to be a blessing. And when I think about it, there have been times when I have heard about someone's ministry, and I thought, *I would love to be a part of that*, but they didn't ask me, and I didn't seek it out. Likewise, most people don't go out of their way to give toward a ministry unless invited, so we have to be proactive in inviting others to join our support team.

I would like you to take a moment and picture some people who might want to be a part of your ministry and pray for them. Not a prayer for God to persuade them to partner with you, but genuinely pray for their hearts and what God is doing in their lives. Before you reach out to someone to share about your ministry, pray. Ask God to go before you when you call someone, write an email, or meet someone. Then, as people come to mind, pray and ask God for guidance in that connection.

The Cold Call

Many of Bryan's most solid connections began with a cold call, meaning he had not met the person he was calling or writing. Some pastors were not receptive to cold calls or emails. They wanted to know if Bryan had a mutual friend or church who had referred him, and they would not meet with him unless he did. Others would at least give him five minutes to hear what he had to say. When people were open to meeting him, God would do amazing things.

Bryan shared a story with me of a cold call turned into a cool connection. This was not a phone call but an in-person attempt at speaking with a pastor. While Bryan was on deputation as a single, he would deliver printed newsletters to different churches in the area. When he brought these letters to a church, he would ask the receptionist if he might speak with a pastor to share his ministry and ask for support. But more importantly, he wanted to build relationships. A few times, he was able to talk with the associate pastor or missions pastor, but there were not many who signed on as ministry partners. But Bryan was faithful to ask despite what he thought the answer might be.

One day, Bryan delivered those newsletters to a church he'd not been to before. Again he was faithful and asked to speak with a pastor. The missions pastor agreed to hear about his ministry. That pastor took a chance on Bryan, and that church became one of his most loyal supporters. That pastor was not just partnering with the ministry; he was partnering with Bryan. And it wasn't just about the financial support; it was about the relationship.

When I met the people at that church, I could feel the genuine love they had for Bryan and their sincere interest in his ministry. They were all so delighted the Lord had brought him a wife, and he would no longer be alone on the mission field. Now, we both have a wonderful relationship with that pastor and many of the people who attend that church.

If you are like me, you may not be a fan of talking on the phone, and you may shy away from calling people you haven't met, but remember, there is value in a cold call. This story, along with many others, shows that a simple phone call, email, or visit can lead to deep relationships if you give it a chance.

The Referral

Not too far removed from a cold call is receiving a referral. This can still feel like a cold call since you are calling or writing someone you haven't met, but at least you can give the name of the person who referred you. For instance, a friend suggested we reach out to Pastor Darrell, who had just taken the senior pastor position at a church in the area. She thought he might be interested in our ministry, so she gave us his name and the name of his church. She didn't have his phone number or an email address, so we had to look it up.

Praying we had found the correct contact information, in faith we sent Darrell an email asking if he would be willing to meet for coffee. He replied with (as much as can be expressed in writing) a resounding yes. We arrived at the coffee shop a little early and made ourselves comfortable in the plush chairs. We enjoyed the aroma of the freshly ground coffee as we prayed and prepared for our meeting.

When Darrell arrived, he flashed a huge grin as he approached us. He gave us each a handshake-into-a-hug greeting and excused himself to get his coffee. Bryan and I looked at each other and grinned, warmed by the love we had already received. Darrell came back with his coffee and settled into another plush chair across from us. His eyes twinkled when he told us he was excited to have received our email. He encouraged us to share our ministry with him.

As we began, he nodded in approval as he hung on every word of every story. His excitement fueled ours, and we kept going as he asked more questions, prompting more stories. Finally, realizing the time was running short, we wanted to hear from Darrell. His tears threatened to fall, and my tears fell freely once he revealed the secret behind his excitement.

It was God.

Darrell had been praying to find an aviation ministry for his church to support. MAF sounded like just what he had been looking for. These connections that were made could only have been orchestrated by God. God had brought this man—who happened to have a heart for mission aviation—to pastor a church that one of our supporters knew of. With a name and a prayer, God established a relationship that is still strong to this day. It is truly amazing what God can do when we step out in faith.

The Reality of Rejection

There is a flip side to everything, right? Sometimes when we make our list of people we are confident would love to support our ministry, we are surprised when they don't. Conversely, many of those we think would not support our ministry surprise us as well. While there will be support, there will also be rejection. There are plenty of books on building ministry and inviting ministry partners. Most of them typically encourage missionaries that the first people they should reach out to should be their friends and colleagues, and I agree. Many books even have a script to follow and suggestions on what to say when you call to set up a meeting.

However, it is important to put people before the script. Usually people can tell when you're following one. Sometimes, when we rely solely on the information, it may inadvertently harm relationships. For example, Bryan had called one of his friends to meet for coffee and share about his ministry. He had followed the format laid out in the book, which instructed him to be up front about why he wanted to meet. Even Bryan felt uncomfortable with it. In hindsight, he figures his friend could tell he was following a script. On the day of the meeting, his friend called to cancel, simply stating that he didn't want to give any money.

It is unclear why his friend wouldn't just meet for coffee anyway. I suppose some people assume that others only want their friendship for what they can get out of it, in this case a pledge for monthly support. But God sees our hearts, and He knows our intentions. Sadly, Bryan hasn't had a relationship with that friend since then. In my opinion, had he met Bryan for coffee and then said no, the relationship could have been spared. Alas, he essentially ended the friendship, which breaks my heart—and I didn't even know him.

While it was sad that a friend walked away, Bryan and I acquired many more friends during deputation. We developed many new relationships and gained an amazing support team. There are many people with whom we have shared our ministry who have not supported us financially. But some of those relationships are the deepest and most meaningful ones we have had in our time overseas. They have sent letters with prayers and many other messages of encouragement. We know we could not have made it through some of the trials we faced without those prayer warriors. Don't let the lack of financial partnerships rob you of the joy of prayer partnerships.

I share about rejection not to discourage you but to encourage you not to fear it. God is so much bigger than the word *no*. If you enter a meeting or a call confident of God's calling on your life and His hand on your ministry, your faith shines like a beacon! People are more drawn to confidence than fear. It is important to be excited about your ministry. Being confident of your call to missions and wanting to share your excitement with others takes the pressure off when asking for support. When others see your excitement and belief in the ministry, they are more likely to want to jump on board.

Of course you need financial support, but you have to trust that God will bring it. It is important that people know it is okay to say no. Just like God will not force anyone to love Him, we can't manipulate people into supporting us. It is imperative that people feel they have a choice and are not coerced into anything, because that type of support will not last very long. God will provide the finances. Besides, the most important support is from those who want to stand by you while you serve overseas.

Relationships Are Key

During our time on deputation, God showed me that we minister to others as we build relationships. As we invited others to partner with us in prayer and financial support, we were given the privilege of praying for them as well. We were invited to walk alongside them in their life journeys as they walked with us in ours. Relationships cultivated on deputation are mutually beneficial for the kingdom of God.

While having a solid financial support network is important when working overseas, prayer relationships are vital. Living cross-culturally is guaranteed to have trials. Jesus says, "I have said these things to you, that in me you may have peace. In the world you will have tribulation. But take heart; I have overcome the world" (John 16:33). Jesus guarantees we will have trouble in the world. He wasn't specific about living in a foreign culture. Still, I dare say there will be even more tribulation living cross-culturally. Knowing people are praying for you will bring the Lord's peace to your life.

Inviting others to partner with your ministry is about more than them praying for you and sending a monthly check. Take time to develop deep connections with others while you are on deputation. You will need relationships with people who are genuinely concerned for your heart and your spirit, those who will ask the hard questions. Those are the people you will be able to call on when the tribulation comes.

God Reveals Our Strengths

During your deputation, you may find yourself wondering about what you bring to your ministry. It may even take a while to figure out your role during your support-raising time. It's important not to put too much pressure on yourself to have everything figured out. It's not just about the phone calls, emails, and presentations. If you allow God to work in your heart and do what comes most naturally to you, He will show you your strengths in the most remarkable ways.

As we neared the end of our deputation time, Bryan shared a scene he witnessed time and time again. Of those who would chat with us after a presentation, the men would typically come up to him and ask him technical questions. They would ask questions about aircraft like "What kind of plane do you fly?" and "What size engine is in that?" While Bryan is a pilot and a mechanic, he is not much for chatting about the mechanical side of things. He'd much rather be talking about flying and witnessing God's creation from his "office in the sky" and the work that gets done using the aircraft. But I digress.

As we cleaned up one morning, he told me that after our presentation, as he was fielding these technical questions, he looked over and saw me chatting with another lady. Both of our faces were wet with tears, and we were hugging one another for probably the sixth time during that single conversation. He told me he marveled at how quickly I could connect with others and that he could never accomplish that. He said, "When you find yourself questioning what you bring to this ministry, I want you to remember this scene. And remind yourself that you can connect with people on a level I never could."

I began seeing how God could uniquely use me as Bryan's partner. I brought an aspect of relationship building to this ministry that had been missing. Before we were married, Bryan was in this ministry alone. God said, "It is not good that the man should be alone; I will make him a helper fit for him" (Genesis 2:18). God established me as that helper fit for my husband. Bryan and I have very different gifts, which complement one another.

As a team, you and your spouse can minister to others more fully than you ever could on your own. And you do not just minister through the organization you are with or the work you are doing but with your lives and how you relate to others. Each of you ministers to different people on different levels—yet another reminder that we are all beautifully broken, and God can use us in the most unexpected ways.

Put It on the Schedule

Traveling, speaking, visiting, and working can be draining mentally, emotionally, physically, and spiritually. After we got settled in at Beth's, our host I mentioned in the last chapter, we chatted with her in her living room. We started talking about the dogs, and we all turned to look at them in the yard just in time to see Austin running full speed toward the house. We stood in disbelief as we noticed he was not slowing down. The next thing we saw was him slamming head first against the glass door in a full-on sprint. He bounced off the glass and stood there, stunned.

Apparently, the effects of changing environments every few days had just smacked him on the head, literally. As his senses returned, he slowly trotted in an I-meant-to-do-that manner to go through the doggy door in the next room. I'm sure the folks down the block could hear the laughter that ensued afterward.

Bryan and I would sometimes feel like Austin must have felt: disoriented from the continual change of environment. We only traveled for a couple of weeks, but everything started blending and looking the same after a while. It makes me wonder how musicians and speakers remember what city they are in. Just as we schedule time in our lives for others, it's vital to schedule in time for ourselves. We can clear our senses with some rest, relaxation, and maybe a little—or a lot—of coffee.

Okay, so what does that look like? Let me share a little tidbit from my friend Emily. She and her husband stayed with some folks they didn't know. After receiving some troubling news from her family, they needed some downtime to process. Here's how they handled that situation:

While my husband and I were in the fundraising phase—traveling and staying with people I didn't know—I received some devastating news from my family back home. My whole world shattered with that one phone call, and here I was on the road, in the middle of engagements. I knew myself well enough to know that I needed space alone to process, cry, breathe, and grieve. My husband called our host family on our way back to their house and asked if we could buy pizza for everyone that evening. He kindly explained we would like to eat on our own as I had just received really hard news. It gave them a night off from hosting, and I had the space I needed to be unguarded. Sometimes you can't predict what might happen while you're on the road; don't be afraid to get creative and improvise to make sure you are taking care of yourself too. (E. Robbert, personal communication, June 3, 2021)

Scheduling in downtime can be as simple as the Robberts excusing themselves from the evening meal for some quiet time. You could even take a walk down the street, or to the nearest park. One family we stayed with was very proactive about helping us wind down, and they offered a list of local trails we could explore. That was amazing! So invite your hosts to provide recommendations on where to go for a little "we time." People are usually happy to offer suggestions and are very rarely offended if you need time away.

It's one thing to notice your need for downtime when things seem overwhelming. The goal is to stay ahead of those overwhelming circumstances. If you mark it on your schedule, "Thursday evening is 'we time,'" you won't be able to schedule other engagements at that time. You will still need to be flexible. If Thursdays are the only days someone can meet, perhaps you change your "we time" appointment to Wednesday. But don't take it out entirely or continue to reschedule it. A simple "I'm sorry; we have a previous engagement this Thursday; how about next Thursday?" will suffice.

As I'm sure you've figured out, deputation is a busy time. As important as it is to schedule your downtime, you should also schedule in goodbyes. But be prepared that not everyone will be in a hurry to meet with you. When it was almost time for us to go overseas, we were surprised there seemed to be a lack of urgency from our friends to meet with us. Though we weren't leaving for a couple of months, what they didn't understand was that we wouldn't be able to squeeze in meeting with all of them in our last two weeks in America.

That was an unexpected hurdle that left us reeling with confusion. Why didn't our friends want to see us? Well, it was not that they didn't want to see us; they just thought they had more time. To remedy that, we had a farewell open house dessert that allowed people to come to say goodbye. It was a last-minute idea, but it served its purpose. And you would do well to plan a not-so-last-minute farewell gathering.

This is another example of clarifying expectations and clearly explaining that your time is limited. It is important to say goodbye well. Sure, your friends want to meet up when you are closer to leaving; that's understandable. But if you want to have a meaningful farewell with them, it would be best to schedule a one-on-one meeting and let them know that you will have a more casual gathering for final goodbyes.

Trusting Him

You may find the concept of deputation daunting at first. There may be fear in reaching out and asking others for support, and the thought of traveling so much may seem overwhelming. But I encourage you to try to see all the benefits that come from this process, above and beyond prayer and financial support. Consider the blessings others desire to offer, and the relationships that will develop. Trust God through the process.

Through all the various aspects of support raising we've covered, your focus must be on God. He will bring just the right support team, and He will orchestrate meaningful encounters. Support raising is a continual task throughout your time in ministry. It is important to stay in contact with your supporters and keep them up to date on your ministry and family life. Your support levels will fluctuate during your time overseas, and you may find yourself seeking more support through your prayer letters. God directs us through all phases of our call to missions, so it is essential to look to Him for our direction and follow

Him. Keep your orbit around Jesus—not your schedule, not how much support you've raised, not how many churches you visit. Trust Him to bring you just the right ministry partnership team.

Reflection:

As you think about the ministry team that you believe God is gathering to support you, consider these questions:

- What fears do you have about relying on others for ministry support?
- What needs to happen in order for you to put your trust in God to bring the perfect support team?

Think about the unique aspects you bring to your marriage and ministry.

- What does it look like for you to build relationships and allow God to work in and through you?
- What are the unique ways God may use you in different aspects of ministry?

Think forward to when it is time to say goodbye.

- How will you clearly communicate with your friends and family regarding the constraints on your time and that you would like to say goodbye well?
- What are some ways you would like to spend your "we time"?
- How will you respond when someone asks to meet when you have "we time" scheduled?

I invite you to pray with me.

Prayer:

Father God, I confess I have fears about inviting ministry partners and relying on others to support our ministry. I pray you would help me overcome those fears. I pray you would touch and prepare the hearts of all those we will be contacting. Help me to trust you to bring the perfect support team. I pray you would work in and through me and that I would keep my heart open for you to reveal the unique gifts I bring to my marriage and ministry. Help me remember that you have called some people to support missions, and I should not rob them of that opportunity. In Jesus's name, I pray, amen.

CHAPTER 5

Being Uprooted

Jesus promises a reward for the sacrifices we make to obey God's calling on our lives.

OUR FRIEND BACKED HIS TRUCK up as close as he could get to the stairs. Thankfully, there was just half a flight of stairs to climb. A steady stream of our friends went back and forth, carrying out boxes and furniture, coming back empty-handed for more. I was directing the foot traffic as best I could, pointing out unmarked boxes that were indeed fragile. As I packed up another box in the bedroom, I heard someone shout from the living room, "Load me up!"

The chaos of moving is not something one simply gets used to, and I won't sugarcoat it and say it gets easier. When Bryan and I were married, moving into our first house was my forty-seventh move (yes, forty-seven moves!). I was thirty-six years old. I moved a lot with my family when I was young. When I joined the military, I moved across the country four times and across the ocean twice. For me, picking up and moving was not that big a deal. Not that I enjoyed it, nor was it easy, but it had become a part of life—change seemed my one constant before I met God.

That much change is not without heartbreak. With every move, I would leave a little piece of myself behind, and I felt like I was always the new kid. I had to learn to adapt, alter, and adjust to new homes, cities, schools, friends, etc. And it took its toll. In each new location,

I would have only one or two close friends. I don't know if I naturally prefer to have only a few friends or if the constant moving made me fearful of reaching out to anyone else. But I do know that my world crumbled a little more each time I had to say goodbye to those friends.

I left for the Navy a month after my eighteenth birthday. Leaving my family broke my heart, but it seemed like the best option for me to have a decent future. Unfortunately, the familiar cycle of pain with goodbye only continued every time I moved with the military. And if I wasn't transferring on orders, my friends were. It was like a revolving door of friendship, and each goodbye left another void in my life. Through those ten years in the service, I learned that if I wanted to have community, I needed to make friends quickly and always be prepared to say goodbye. But it never got easier.

When I was ten years out of the military, I had found a great church, made some great friends, and had a great support system. I believed I was finished with the constant moving and saying goodbye, and I could work on laying down roots. I thought I was on my way to a stable life. But here I was again. The Lord had called me into missions, and Bryan and I were preparing to go overseas. The purpose behind the upcoming goodbyes made more sense than those in the military, but they *felt* more difficult.

Letting Go

Bryan and I met with his mom for dinner for one of many goodbyes to come. We sat and watched with anticipation to see her response to the gift we gave her. It was early February; it wasn't a holiday or her birthday, so this gift came as quite a surprise. Bryan and I held hands as she carefully peeled back the wrapping paper. She picked up the tiny little hat to reveal two tiny little socks. Her face went from perplexed to shocked! She looked up at us. "A baby?" she exclaimed as her tears wet the wrapping paper still sitting in her lap. No more words would come, only hugs and joyous tears.

Two weeks later, this soon-to-be grandma called us. She was frantic. We made the two-hour drive to her house as fast as we could legally go. When we arrived, Mom had calmed down from the hysterics we had heard on the phone, and now she sat in stoic disbelief. Police surrounded her home, and an ambulance was waiting outside. She had not called us to talk about the joyous discovery we had shared two weeks earlier. Her husband, Bryan's stepfather, had suddenly passed away.

The weight of this goodbye pressed into the depths of our hearts. Bryan's mom was going to be alone for the first time in over thirty years, and we were just months away from moving overseas. In addition, I was carrying her first grandchild. When it was just us saying goodbye, it seemed more bearable. Now we were faced with the reality that our baby would spend much of his life not knowing his Nana, and she wouldn't know him. We knew we were doing what God had called us to do, but my heart still grieved that we wouldn't be around family and that we were leaving Bryan's mom at such a difficult season of her life.

There is little doubt that you are excited for what is to come in your missions journey. But if you haven't felt it already, you may begin to feel a little tug at your heart, a niggling that makes you wonder if you are making the right decision. Likely, you may already feel turmoil in your heart when you think of everyone and everything you will be leaving behind.

A mixture of emotions comes with any transition. There is sadness for what will be left behind on top of joy for what's to come. Therefore, it is essential to keep communication open within your family, especially for children. Being open to talking about things you will miss and things you are looking forward to allows you to process the emotions rather than stuffing them down as if they are not allowed.

Maybe you wonder how well you will adapt to being away from extended family or, if you have children, how well they will adjust. Perhaps you have family members who are advanced in years, and you feel you may be neglecting your obligation to care for them. Maybe you have siblings assuming that task, and you wonder if they will feel abandoned or burdened by your departure. Perhaps you find yourself passing on your work tasks to someone else, and you are feeling a sense of putting a burden on your coworkers as well.

Entering into missions to spread the good news of Jesus comes at a cost. But we find hope in the Word of God. In the book of Genesis, the Lord called Abram to leave his home and family but promised to bless him and the nations through him for doing so.

> Now the Lord said to Abram, "Go from your country and your kindred and your father's house to the land that I will show you. And I will make of you a great nation, and I will bless you and make your name great, so that you will be a blessing. I will bless those who bless you, and him who dishonors you I will curse, and in you all the families of the earth shall be blessed." (Genesis 12:1–3)

God didn't even tell Abram where he was going, just that He would show him when it was time. But he would bless the nations through him.

Jesus also promises a glorious reward for the sacrifices we make to obey the calling God has put on our lives. He said to his disciples,

> Truly, I say to you, in the new world, when the Son of Man will sit on his glorious throne, you who have followed me will also sit on twelve thrones, judging the twelve tribes of Israel. And *everyone who has left houses or brothers or sisters or father or mother or children or lands, for my name's sake, will receive a hundredfold and will inherit eternal life*. But many who are first will be last, and the last first. (Matthew 19:28–30)

Jesus promises us we will receive a *hundredfold* what we sacrifice, and we will inherit eternal life.

It is not easy to leave family and friends. Trust in the Lord to help you through these adjustments and goodbyes. He will be with you, and go before you, just as He said to Moses, "My presence will go with you, and I will give you rest" (Exodus 33:14). Your fears are natural and to be expected. It is necessary to pray through them and listen for God's voice in all your circumstances.

You may say, "But Mari, I'm not as concerned for us as for the ones we're leaving behind. How do we help them understand? How do we help them cope with goodbye?" The void left in the hearts of those we love will never be filled by anyone else. It is a "you-shaped" hole. If you can help your family see what you are going to be a part of, and they can see the good that lies in front of you, they will be better equipped to let you go with their blessing. Bryan's mom saw the importance of our ministry and sent us off with her blessing.

That's why it's so important, as I mentioned in my last chapter, that you make it a point to say goodbye well. Relationships can stay intact if we emphasize their significance. It would be prudent to make a list of people you absolutely must meet in person to say goodbye. You would do well to also have a secondary and tertiary list. This will help you schedule visits and ensure no one gets missed. Taking the time to express to someone how important they are in your life shows them that they matter to you. That gives more incentive to stay in contact.

Once you move overseas, there may be times you feel isolated and very alone. After being on the field for about a year, it felt like friends in our home culture had forgotten us. We knew they still loved us—that wasn't a question—but as they changed and their families grew, and we changed and our family grew, life just kept going for all of us. Things got busy, and since our friends weren't there to share it, sometimes we felt lonely. When we went on home assignment, we reconnected as if nothing had changed, but things had changed. We just had to adjust to who we had all become. It's important to be intentional about staying connected with those who mean the most to you.

We are blessed to have technology that missionaries who served before us didn't. We can stay connected with family and friends through email, social media, or video calling. So while hugs, meeting for coffee, birthday and office parties, and holiday gatherings will be missed, at least the lines of communication can stay open.

Paring Down

It may be a no-brainer to say it is difficult to say goodbye to family and friends, but what about belongings? Our things? Our stuff? While our friends were shuttling our boxes out of my apartment, it occurred to me that not all moves are created equal. When people move within a state, say across town or to a nearby city, they would likely have friends who could help them pack up a truck and move all their stuff to their new place. However, if they move across the country, things are a little more involved. They may have friends to help them in one location, but unless they are moving back to something or someone, they may not have a band of friends to help on the other side.

When I was in the military and received orders to Hawaii, I did two overseas moves, meaning my stuff went by boat across the ocean to Hawaii, then it went by boat again back to the continental United States. Both times, it was pretty straightforward. The military movers packed all my stuff, loaded it in a big crate, shipped it, and I had a Navy base on the receiving side. But moving overseas for missions? To a foreign country? That's a whole different ball game.

When you sign on for mission work, you can't just pack up *all* your stuff and go. You must determine what is essential and take only the bare minimum. Since Bryan had already pared down his belongings four years earlier, we only had my stuff. After forty-seven moves, I thought I had pared down my life to be pretty minimal, but once we started to sort through my things, that was far from accurate. I might have more than just a *digital* hoarding issue.

I had not realized how much sentimental value I had placed on the stuff in my life until we began taking pictures of all of it to post to an online garage sale site. Then we opened our doors to allow a slew of strangers to parade through our home, rummage through my things, and negotiate their way down to a reasonable-for-them price. More than a few times I cried as I watched strangers driving away with my treasures, wondering if they would care about them as much as I did.

At one point during our estate sale, I left Bryan in charge and went to get coffee for us. When I came back, Bryan excitedly informed me that he had sold my motorcycle helmet. It was essentially brand new. I had worn it maybe a handful of times, and I had paid nearly $300 for it. I asked Bryan how much he sold it for, and he said $50. That man just got the deal of a lifetime on a helmet, and I wept.

Something I gleaned from that sale is that things are just things. After selling off most of my belongings, I learned that some missionaries would donate all their belongings and trust God to provide what they needed. Looking back, it might have been better—and easier—for us to donate my things. After that sale, I promised myself I would not get emotionally attached to the stuff we would accumulate overseas. I knew we would not likely be taking any of it back to America with us when that time came. Things like the rocking chair we would ship for us to rock our expected son or the dining room table we would share meals over as a family. Things like the living room table that would double as our son's first dancing stage and would hold our feet as we enjoyed movies and popcorn. Things like the Christmas tree I would so desperately want so that our summer Christmas would have some sense of tradition. They are all just things.

I know that parting with belongings can be difficult for many people. If this is difficult for you, I pray that the Lord will walk with you as you sort through your things. Plan to sort through your stuff sooner rather than later and determine what you can and cannot live without. If you are uncertain about parting with something, this will give you time to think about it. Try to pare down as much as possible before moving overseas. The last-minute packing can be hectic, and you may end up missing things you need and packing those you don't.

Contact someone currently serving in your host country to see if you can find the items you need there. Your soon-to-be teammates may have a list of things you will need and know whether you can buy them in your host country or if you need to ship them. In addition, your organization should let you know how much shipping allowance you have and help you organize your shipment.

I pray that the Lord will give you a sense of peace, knowing that whatever you choose to sell or donate will go to someone in need, and it will be well received. Moving, paring down, and packing up is not easy. But with change comes a chance to start fresh and open up your heart to new possibilities. I hope that you are encouraged to see what God has in store.

Packing Up

When you do get a packing list, please remember that it is just a guide. You don't have to get everything on the list. You know yourself and what you will need and want. If loaf pans are on the list, and you've never baked bread in your life and don't intend to start, don't worry about it; just cross it off. And if you need or want something that is not on the list, add it! And ask if you can get it in your host country.

For example, when Bryan was preparing to move overseas the first time, he was single. He received a packing list for his program that had been written by one of the wives. Many of the suggested items to pack were of the cooking and baking variety. You may not know this, but Bryan is a follow-the-rules kind of guy; perhaps that's why he's such a great pilot. But being that he didn't know anything about Lesotho, he just did what he was told and got the items on the list. That included items like loaf pans, cookie sheets, and other kitchen items. Bryan didn't cook, let alone bake. Those things were never used until we moved overseas together. Also on the list was long underwear. I won't go into my husband's undergarment preferences. Suffice it to say I've never known him to wear long underwear. Still, he got them because they were on the list! Don't be a slave to the list!

For one of the families preparing to join our program, we set up a WhatsApp group with all of the wives on our team. While this soon-to-be team member was paring down her belongings and deciding what she needed, she could ask us if she could get those things in the country. Being aware of what you need, and having the means to ask someone who can just pop over to the market and look for that, is *huge*.

As I said earlier, connect with someone currently serving where you are going, not someone who lived there five years ago. In the eighteen months Bryan was away from Lesotho when we married, another mall had gone up across town. So much more was available since he had lived there, but we didn't ask, and we shipped things we could have gotten in the country.

Embrace the Changes

As I reflect on the story I shared earlier about how many times I've moved, I picture a little girl with a tally sheet, making a tick mark each time the moving van pulled up. That's not how it happened. In fact, by the time I was eighteen, I had lost count of our moves. But I was talking to a friend one day who had spent her whole life in one place. She and I were polar opposites on the moving spectrum. Where her parents had settled, there she was raised. She lived in the same place her entire life, the same city, even the same house! I could not even begin to imagine what that must have been like. And when I told her I had moved a lot, she asked how many times I'd moved. I didn't have a number, but I knew it was pretty high.

After that conversation, I was curious. *How many times have I moved?* So I compiled a list. At first, I just wanted to see if I could remember all the places I'd lived, but then, memories of the changes I went through during those moves began to surface as well. When I reached the final count, it turned into a badge of honor kind of thing. One of those things where I could raise my hand when someone asked who in the room thinks they have moved the most—though I've yet to hear that question asked.

I mentioned that change had seemed the one constant in my life and not necessarily in a good way. I have since come to embrace change as a constant, but now it is coupled with the unchanging, unwavering love of God. Embracing change has served me well for life in general, but especially as a missionary. The seasons of life are continually changing. So we can't expect things to stay the same overseas any more than we would expect them to stay the same in America.

One missionary friend I interviewed said it best:

Don't expect things to stay the same. In your role, on your team, with your family, with your heart. Seasons are always changing. No kids, kids, empty nest. Team needs or dynamics. Your own desires, capacity, or health, will all change at some point. So, as you dream of what life will be like, expect that it will vary. When you are uncomfortable with your current scenario, I hope you find some purpose and joy in it. But know it isn't forever. When you are thrilled with what life looks like, enjoy it to the fullest while it lasts. Hold it gently, though. It is not the end of the story either. (K. Martin, personal communication, May 8, 2021)

It's Not Just about Them

As you serve overseas, you will be stretched in ways you've never imagined. Embracing change and being able to adapt, alter, and adjust is more than just a coping mechanism. Nothing in life stays the same. Children grow, parents die, friends move, and jobs change or cease to exist. Everything is ever changing. As it says in Ecclesiastes 3:1 (KJV), "To every thing there is a season, and a time to every purpose under the heaven." I believe—and I've heard this from countless missionaries including my husband—that going overseas in missions usually begins as a quest to reach people with the gospel of Christ. However, the ones God usually reaches and transforms the most are the missionaries themselves.

As I talked with Bryan one night, he shared about the beginning of his journey into missions. As he reflected, he confessed to having somewhat of a God complex when he arrived in Lesotho. In his mind, he was going to transform the lives of everyone in the mountains of Lesotho with the gospel of Christ. However, he would often arrive home in the evening frustrated at the lack of change or the apathy he would encounter during the day.

Bryan told me that this "God complex" was fueled during deputation. He said,

I strived to communicate how *important* and *needed* MAF's ministry was in Lesotho. As I did that, the belief that began to develop in my heart was that *I* was important and needed in this ministry. Over time, the Lord graciously showed me some of the wrong attitudes I had. I began to realize that God didn't need me to rescue Lesotho; He's certainly capable of doing that without me! However, God was *inviting* me to become a part of His kingdom's work which is much larger and more extravagant than I could have imagined. I also realized that God was more interested in who I was *becoming* and less interested in what I *felt* like I was *accomplishing*. (B. Eygabroad, personal communication, May 18, 2021)

As you grow in your life with Christ through your service overseas, you will gain an appreciation for God and life unlike any other. Kathleen shares again,

Expect God to do amazing things! Yes, in the ministry around you, but often the biggest work is in your own heart. He will grow you (expect growing pains). Be eager in the midst to see the person God is going to make you into. In my experience, it was rarely pleasant (though, sometimes!) But the heartache, stretching, and challenges did bring me closer to God and, hopefully, made me more and more into the image of Christ. (K. Martin, personal communication, May 8, 2021)

Rooted in Christ

Embracing change and welcoming the uprooting of our lives goes against the grain for so many people. So many people have this notion that they need to buy a home, settle down, and lay down some roots. It is important to realize that, like our identity, our roots are in Christ, not in the pleasures or comforts of the world. We can make a comfortable home, community, and routine anywhere Jesus calls us to serve. But we are not fueled or fed by those things alone. Our roots are in

God, and our nourishment comes from Him. Jesus says, "I am the vine; you are the branches. Whoever abides in me and I in him, he it is that bears much fruit, for apart from me you can do nothing" (John 15:5).

Settling down and trying to conform to any culture is not from God.

> Do not love the world or the things in the world. If anyone loves the world, the love of the Father is not in him. *For all that is in the world*—the desires of the flesh and the desires of the eyes and pride of life—*is not from the Father but is from the world*. And the world is passing away along with its desires, but whoever does the will of God abides forever. (1 John 2:15–17 ESV)

Embracing change, especially in the areas God is working on in your heart, can be the most God-honoring thing you do. Accept His invitation to His kingdom work. Keep your eyes open to see all the marvelous works He is doing in you and around you. Keep your focus on your relationship with your Creator, and the work He wants you to do will pour out through that.

Reflection:

With the American culture emphasizing putting down roots, think about letting that go.

- What feelings rise up in you when you think about being uprooted?
- In what areas do you need to shift your focus to be more rooted in Christ?

Think about your friends, family, and coworkers you will be leaving behind.

- Who would you like to meet with to say goodbye?
- What do you need to do now to arrange meetings with them?

Think about your stuff, the items you use every day and those you have in storage.

- What will you need to adjust in order to pare down to the bare essentials?

- What belongings do you have sentimental value attached to?
- As you are paring down and packing up, what steps do you need to take to be in contact with someone in your future host country who can help you decide what to bring? Think about the transformation ahead.
- What is your response to missionaries being transformed more than those they strive to reach?
- What are you expecting God to do in the lives of those to whom you minister?
- What are you expecting God to do in your life?

I invite you to pray with me.

Prayer:

Father God, I confess my fear of the unknown. I don't know what lies ahead, but you do. I pray you would prepare the hearts of those we will be leaving behind and help us say goodbye well to those we love. I pray you would help me embrace change as a constant of life and help me pair that with your unchanging goodness and strength. Please prepare my heart for the work you plan to do in me. Remind me that being uprooted from the world and rooted in you is where you want me to be.

CHAPTER 6

Your Best You

*The stress and newness of an international move decrease the
capacity of the coping mechanisms you've put in place to block out
painful wounds of the past.*

GROWING UP, I WAS A very emotional child. It didn't take much
to make me cry. It still doesn't. Don't put on a Hallmark movie
without tissues nearby! But as a child, I never felt the freedom
to express my emotions. More than once, others said to me, "Don't be
so emotional." So I tried not to be. Instead I continually stuffed my
feelings until I exploded in a rage, setting into motion a vicious cycle
of stuffing and exploding. Each stuffed feeling added more gunpow-
der to an emotional powder keg. Each swallowed fear snipped the
fuse shorter and shorter until it reached the ignition point—one tiny,
seemingly insignificant event sparking just enough to blow the whole
barrel to bits.

Let's fast-forward to when I had been overseas for nearly two
years. There I was, in the baby aisle of the grocery store, mindlessly
examining the packages of teething snacks as my toddler sat in the
shopping cart playfully investigating all the groceries he could reach.
The mom-to-be couldn't have known what my reaction would be when
she walked by us with her round belly. I didn't even realize how it
would affect me or that it would affect me. My eyes were transfixed
as I watched her lovingly rub her tummy as she examined a package

of newborn diapers. Then, out of instinct, my hand went to my now empty but still-too-large tummy, and the dam broke. Tears flooded my face as thoughts of what might have been flooded my mind.

Months of trying to keep my emotions under control had finally caught up with me. I had a feeling God had brought this woman into my path for such a time as this, and that was precisely what I needed. She had no idea what role she was playing in my life, but God did. So I stood for what seemed to be an eternity, and I let the tears come as my son played with the banana package, seemingly oblivious of his mommy's meltdown occurring in front of him.

I regained enough composure to maneuver the shopping cart to the checkout till and paid for my groceries. As I loaded groceries into the car and buckled my son into his car seat, a second wave of tears and emotions caught me by surprise, accompanied by sobs and other unattractive facial leakages. I dug in the diaper bag for the baby wipes and sat behind the steering wheel crying an ugly cry. Finally a horn sounded, snapping me out of my breakdown. I wiped my face and took a deep breath. I started the car and went straight home to reach out to a counselor. It was time to talk. I had held it in longer than I should have, and now it had negatively impacted my daily life.

There was something deeper going on in my heart that I needed to address. I had suffered a loss, but I was not allowing myself to grieve it. A part of me had died, but I was not allowing myself to mourn it. A dream had disintegrated, and I was pushing away any hope of dreaming again. Those stuffed emotions came to the surface just because I saw a woman who was about to have something I had lost.

Emotional Health

I have covered quite a bit about knowing who you are in Christ and some practical aspects of your missionary journey. However, before we continue into even more spiritual and practical perspectives, I want to address one critical factor in adjusting to missionary life: you. With all the emotions, changes, and upheavals that go hand in hand with going into missions, significant emotional and spiritual aspects are unique to each missionary's journey.

I am not here to dig up old bones, but I want you to think about your emotional triggers, even if they are hard to think about. Making an international move and living in a culture different from the one you know is stressful. Yes, it is full of joy and excitement, but the stress and newness also decrease the capacity of the coping mechanisms you've put in place to block out painful wounds of the past. Therefore, it is important to know your triggers and have a plan in place for when they are activated. You'll be better prepared and less likely to be blindsided when these emotional moments occur while you're serving in missions.

What has happened in your life that has caused such emotional turmoil that someone simply walking by could trigger a response in you? What scents might trigger fears deep in your soul? What song brings you back to a time in your life you would rather forget? What food makes you gag because it probes a painful memory?

You are about to embark on a journey of living uprooted. It is beneficial to know your triggers, weaknesses, and your insecurities. If you know what's happening when the tears start flowing seemingly all of a sudden, then you can reach out to someone to help you work through them. If you start working through your emotions before going on the field, you will better handle the other effects of living overseas.

During our time overseas, we experienced much heartache and loss. In the first two years alone we were newly married, moved overseas, and had our first child in a foreign country, having only been there five months. I had two more surgeries after my cesarean section and lost a beloved pet. This first miscarriage happened just a year after our first son was born. Two years later I experienced another miscarriage just two weeks before we were scheduled to go on home assignment. I will share more about all of that in a later chapter.

I needed help coping with all the tragedy we had endured in our first year, and now, adding to that, the pain of this first miscarriage tipped me over the emotional edge, and I did not have a counselor on standby. I went many months trying to keep my feelings in check. I would try to be strong for my not-yet-two-year-old and my husband, swallowing my emotions like oatmeal on a full stomach just to make it through the day. I ensured my son was fed, got dinner on the table, and counted down the hours until I could crawl in bed and escape reality with sleep. There was no living going on inside me. I was empty. I was spent.

Unfortunately, I didn't reach out for help until I was amid an emotional breakdown. At times I thought I was going crazy. I was losing my mental capacity for simple daily tasks, and some of my behavior scared me. I wish I would have had someone I could reach out to. Instead, I began to feel like a burden to my family and the friends on my team. Each time I expressed my sadness, I felt as if others were tired of hearing it. I felt like they were expecting me to move on and get over it, but that was easier said than done. The trauma of losing a child is not something I could simply get over, nor was it easy to move on.

Consider Counseling

When I did finally connect with a counselor, the suggestions he had for me worked wonders for my heart and mind. For example, he suggested daily quiet time to reflect and process the day's events, keeping a journal to document feelings and prayers, and physical activity to actively process my emotions—thus reconnecting my spirit, mind, and body. We established a trustful connection, and I could call on him when things began to feel overwhelming again.

Perhaps you believe that going to a counselor is a sign of weakness. Unfortunately, many people feel that way. Maybe you think since you are going into missions, you are supposed to have it all together. Let me tell you; missionaries are some of the most broken people I know. But they have the capacity to be vulnerable, open, and authentic, which allows them to connect and minister to others. There is no shame at all in getting counseling. Taking the opportunity to be open and honest in the safe space of a counselor's office allows you to discover what you can be open and vulnerable about in ministry.

Meeting with a Christian counselor regularly *before* going overseas allows you and the counselor to establish a trusting relationship in a healthy, stable environment before you are in an emotional upheaval. Many counselors can help you discover what emotions you need to work through before you immerse yourself into life overseas, which is bound to be fraught with difficulties of its own but may also include triggers for your emotional state. Then the two of you can identify areas that may become problematic and develop an action plan for if something should happen to trigger a response. Finding a counselor who can help you work through issues before moving overseas allows you to have someone to connect with when things get challenging on the field.

Mental Health

Knowing your emotional triggers is essential to your mental health. The two are intertwined. As one who prides herself on efficiency, especially since becoming a mom, it's highly probable I will find myself trying to juggle more than one thing at a time during the day. Unfortunately, trying to get too many things done at once can send me reeling into very dangerous places. I used to pride myself on my ability to juggle many tasks, but now it was a recipe for emotional and mental disaster. I needed to focus on fewer things at a given time.

Over the last twenty years or so, there has been a lot of scrutiny on multitasking. While many people claim to be good at it, especially moms, multitasking is not actually focusing well on many things at once. But rather, it's the ability to quickly shift focus from one task to another during a given time frame. Depending on the task, the belief that we are good at multitasking could set us up for failure in that we may not focus on getting one job done well and moving onto the next but try to get many tasks done well enough before the day's end.

An article from the Cleveland Clinic says,

Another pitfall [of multitasking] is that trying to do too much at once makes it harder to be mindful and truly present in the moment—and mindfulness comes with a plethora of benefits for our minds and our bodies. In fact, many therapies based on mindfulness can even help patients suffering from depression, anxiety, chronic pain and other conditions.[1]

So focus on one task at a time, and leave the multitasking to dinner-time, when you must shift your focus to different aspects of a three-part meal and step over or around children in the kitchen. Your mental health will thank you for it.

While multitasking takes its toll on our mental clarity, focusing too long on one task can also lead to mental fatigue. There is something to be said for taking a mental break if you have been focusing on one thing for an extended period of time.[2] For that matter, taking time away from tasks, in general, is good for our mental health as well.

Once I spoke with a counselor after my meltdown in the grocery store, I began taking an hour each day for myself. In the beginning, I typically took time during my son's early rest time, but sometimes it was nice to have it in the evening to process the day's events. Once our son was in bed for the night, and my husband was working on a project, I would find a quiet place to unwind, turn off all my electronic devices, limit all the potential distractions, and reconnect to myself and God.

Over the years, as my son has grown and we added a child through adoption, my quiet time began to shift, but it was precious enough that I made it a point to keep it in my schedule. Since I never really got our son off his nap schedule and our daughter still needed daily naps, we implemented a two-hour block of quiet time right after lunch. During that time, the kids either sleep or do a quiet activity, such as reading, and I get to work and have my own quiet time. If you don't have a regular quiet time in your schedule, I highly suggest implementing one. You can start with just ten or fifteen minutes and work your way up to the desired amount of time. It is a glorious respite in the middle of the day.

Perhaps you are like me and many other women, and you feel guilty for even taking a shower, let alone taking time away from your family just for an hour of quiet. Maybe finding the time and a quiet place is challenging in itself. Children, your spouse, neighbors, friends, and electronics can all distract from quality quiet time. The more I thought about what led up to my emotional distress, the more I realized that I would be of no use to anyone if I didn't take that time. So I determined it was better to lose an hour with my family than to lose my mind. Choose a time when these distractions will be minimal and request to be left undisturbed during that time. Don't wait until there is a problem to reach out for help. Take steps now to put preventive measures into effect so you won't be scrambling when issues arise. Make it happen. You are worth it.

Nutritional Health

Recently, when I woke up one morning in late March, I pulled the covers off, and the chill of the African fall air rushed over my skin. I did a mental assessment of my body and grimaced as I rolled over to check the clock. I closed my eyes and prayed, "Lord, no more, please." I willed myself out of bed and hobbled to the bathroom. I looked in the mirror but didn't recognize myself. My face looked ashen and dry. How did I age so quickly? Just five months ago, I looked and felt ten years younger. I was running regularly, eating well, and now I could barely get out of bed, let alone walk or run.

I lumbered into the kitchen, where Bryan was preparing breakfast. My kids ran to say good morning, my three-year-old daughter with outstretched arms begging me to pick her up. "Not now, sweetheart. Mommy hurts."

My seven-year-old son asked, "Mommy, are we going for a walk today?"

"Not today, bud. Mommy hurts." I choked back tears as I watched both of my kids walk away with their heads hung down and their bottom lips poked out.

This pain had been going on for five months, and it was only getting worse. Now it was affecting my family, my ability to enjoy life with my kids, and even my cognition—I couldn't focus for more than a few minutes on a task. Seemingly overnight, I had gone from running six days a week to wincing in pain just to stand up. Every joint in my body hurt—literally—even the joints of my spine. The pain had become way too familiar and very unwelcome. In addition, my belly was constantly bloated and distended; however, I hadn't gained a lot of weight, so I thought my diet was acceptable and that there must be a deeper medical issue.

As I researched my symptoms, I began to notice a pattern. Many of the articles that came up in my searches discussed foods that cause inflammation. Having been a personal trainer, I knew a little something about maintaining a healthy diet. But I didn't know much, if anything, about inflammatory foods. Though it seemed to have happened overnight, it actually happened over the holidays when all the yummy treats just kept coming. That was the time I began slowly poisoning my body.

By February, though I stopped enjoying so many sweet confections, I started making bread and pizza dough and having half a cola with our pizza night every week, etc. I started looking more closely at the sugar content of the seemingly healthy granola bars I would have for a snack, and I realized I consumed a fair amount of refined sugar every day of the week. These are just a few foods that were wreaking havoc on my body. While I enjoyed these things in what I thought to be moderation, I was daily bombarding my body with what it was treating as toxins to the point it could no longer function properly. It had no recourse but to fight. When our bodies fight, they fight with inflammation.

I took the information I found in a few different places and combined it to fit what I needed. First, I began intermittent fasting to allow my body time to respond to the inflammation before bombarding it with more inflammatory ingredients. Next, it was time to take out the culprits. I took out the sugar first. After about a week, I thought

I might be feeling a little better, but it wasn't enough. So the next week I took out all grains, including corn. Now it was all gone—the grains and the sugar, gone. There was no more pizza, pasta, cola, other confections, or comfort foods.

Within a week, my life changed! Within a week, I was virtually pain free! Within a week, I was getting up without wincing. I was able to go on two three-hour hikes during a weekend getaway with my family—without pain! Two weeks later, I went on a five-hour trek through the mountains—to be precise, over the mountains—with a girlfriend. Besides the typical muscle pain that kind of exercise induces, I was completely pain free! Two days after that, I was able to run again! I was able to lift my daughter without pain! My son and I enjoyed our walks again, and I remained pain free!

This experience opened my eyes! The poor choices I was making in my diet affected more than just my physical body; they affected my mental clarity, my emotional well-being, and my spiritual connection with God. We humans, ingeniously designed by the Master Creator, are holistic beings. Just as I mentioned earlier that our emotions are intertwined with our minds, both are intertwined with our physical bodies.

It is essential to have the proper perspective concerning health. When December comes, I may miss out on some delectably tasty Christmas treats. But for my body's sake and for the sake of being present for my family, I am fully convinced that grains and sugar do not belong inside me! In that case, I don't think I'll be *missing* anything at all.

I don't consider this new way of eating restrictive, but freeing! I do not want to sacrifice my health and wellness for a few cookies. Just because others enjoy confections, seemingly without issue, does not mean that's the right choice for me. Just as Paul says,

> "All things are lawful for me," but *not all things are help-ful.* "All things are lawful for me," but *I will not allow food to dominate me.* "Food is meant for the stomach and the

stomach for food"—and God will destroy both one and the other. (1 Corinthians 6:12–13)

Perhaps you've been struggling with unexplainable pain, fuzzy cognition, or other ways your body just doesn't feel right. In that case, I encourage you to examine your diet and ensure the choices you are making are doing your body good. Even if you are not experiencing pain, it is still good to investigate what foods may cause adverse reactions and those that commonly cause inflammation and replace them with natural foods that promote good health.

Physical Health

Now that we've covered emotional health, mental health, and nutrition, let's tie it all together with these magnificent vessels God developed for us to use—our bodies. In addition to allowing ourselves an emotional outlet, mental rest, and the right foods, it is also imperative that we give our physical bodies rest and movement. I talk a little more about rest in my chapter on travel. For now, I want to discuss the importance of exercise.

Please stick with me here. From my experience as a personal trainer and physical therapist assistant, I know that the word *exercise* is like a curse word to some people! I've heard all the PT jokes, from "personal torturer" to "pain therapy." But finding the proper exercise for you, one you will enjoy and look forward to, is possible! Sticking with them overseas can be tricky, though. For instance, my exercise of choice is running. While I could run outside the first couple of years overseas, safety concerns heightened, and traffic worsened. Thus it was no longer safe to be running on the streets—and sidewalks are hard to come by. We saved up for me to buy a treadmill, and I use it regularly, but that may not be an option for some.

Many missionaries go overseas fearing exotic diseases. But a few years ago, when we went to the doctor for our checkups, the doctor told us that the most common ailments of missionaries returning from the mission field were still problems associated with obesity, poor diet, and lack of exercise. And she was correct. According to the World Health Organization (WHO), "The world's biggest killer is ischemic heart disease, responsible for 16% of the world's total deaths. Since 2000, the largest increase in deaths has been for this disease, rising by more than 2 million to 8.9 million deaths in 2019."[3]

Finding the right exercise program for you benefits more than just your physical fitness. Physical activity for just thirty minutes a day helps your body holistically—as in emotionally, mentally, and physically. I'm sure you have heard it said that exercise releases endorphins. Well, it does. In addition to giving you that overall sense of well-being (physical), endorphins may help to alleviate depression (emotional) and reduce stress and anxiety (mental).

You may already have a regular exercise routine in place. Wonderful! Could you adjust that to be compatible with your new life overseas? Some things to think about would be access to the internet, electricity, and safety. If you do not have a routine in place, you can purchase fitness plans on DVD that combine strength and cardio exercise in a thirty-minute program. I have used the P90X3 videos, and the results were fantastic.

Temple of God

To be your best, you must care for all dimensions of yourself. "Or do you not know that your body is a temple of the Holy Spirit within you, whom you have from God? You are not your own, for you were bought with a price. So glorify God in your body" (1 Corinthians 6:19–20).

In your spiritual life, be in continual prayer with God for guidance for the other aspects of life. For example, pray for discernment in your emotional life and finding the right counselor. Pray for guidance in your mental life, establishing a regular quiet time and prioritizing tasks. And be in prayer for your physical health, to maintain or develop healthy eating and exercise habits. Having all these resources and habits in place frees up your mind and allows you to grow and learn as you move forward in your missionary journey.

Reflection:
Think about some things that have happened to you that may be triggered.
- What are some things that may activate those triggers?
- What has happened in your past that may affect how you address emotions today?

Think about a counselor or mentor you've been working with, or that you might work with.
- Who can you connect with today to begin working through some of these emotional events?
- What methods will you use to keep in contact with your counselor or mentor while you live overseas?

Think about your daily routine and schedule.
- What are some things you can put into place to maintain mental clarity?
- Where can you adjust your schedule to give yourself thirty minutes of quiet time each day?

Think about your nutritional health.
- What are some ideas for maintaining or establishing healthy eating habits?
- What comfort foods might you decide to give up or limit for the sake of overall health?
- What will you need to alter in order to make healthy choices in your new host country?

Think about your physical health.
- How will you need to adjust your fitness routine to be replicated overseas?
- Is your routine memorized, on DVD, or downloaded?
- Will you still be able to access your routine if there is no internet or power?

I invite you to pray with me.

Prayer:

Father God, I confess I have some emotional wounds that could be triggered, especially while living in a new culture. I pray you would help me find someone who can help me heal from these wounds and walk with me as I venture into missionary life overseas. I pray your Holy Spirit will guide me to the right counselor and we can establish a good relationship now while I am stable. And when something happens to shake my emotional state, I can call on them to walk through it with me. I pray for your help as I examine my fitness routine and eating habits to keep my physical health at its best. Thank you for your guidance, wisdom, and strength. I pray in Jesus's name, amen.

CHAPTER 7

Time to Fly

Planning for what we can and allowing margin for the unexpected gives a sense of security when things happen that are out of our control.

W E GATHERED AROUND THE TRUCK outside our friends' home. Tim and Mindy had welcomed us to stay with them for our last month in Washington. All of us felt like we were family. These seemed to be the final days of feeling nomadic as we finally loaded up to head to the airport. Rain threatened to fall that overcast afternoon in Snohomish. We prayed it would hold off just a little longer. I stood by, once again directing foot traffic, as our eight totes—our max baggage allowance for an international humanitarian flight—were loaded into the truck. Being four months pregnant, no one would let me lift anything (and I was okay with that).

That old familiar void began to make its presence known as we said goodbye to Tim and Mindy and their five boys. We loaded in the truck and headed to the airport. After we checked our bags, we had a little extra time to have coffee with Dan (you met him in Chapter 1) and his wife, Ileana, at the airport—another last-minute goodbye. When it came time for us to make our way through security, a lump formed in my throat as I hugged my friend, and I didn't bother trying to hold back the tears.

By the time we got to our gate, I was a hot mess. No amount of cold water splashed on my face could conceal the redness and swelling. Bryan's dad worked for the airlines, so he could come through security and see us off at our gate. Another nice treat and last-minute goodbye. As much as I loved squeezing in the extra few minutes of love, the sound of our boarding call was a welcome one. I needed to be done with goodbye.

Now was the time to focus on getting to the other side of the world. After another round of last-minute hugs, we gathered our bags and headed down the Jetway. The first leg of our forty-two-hour journey had begun. Yes, you read that correctly, forty-two hours door to door.

Surviving or Thriving

Traveling overseas can be a long, arduous journey, but there are some things you can do to minimize exhaustion and stress. Planning for what you can and allowing a margin for the unexpected can give you a great sense of security when things happen that are out of your control. When you allow yourself to expect the unexpected, you are less of a target for spiritual attacks. When you get the practical details taken care of, you are better able to focus on the spiritual.

Before we move on to some of the practicalities of traveling, let's talk about spiritual attack. I will go deeper into this in a later chapter, but it should be touched on here. The term *spiritual attack* gets a lot of scrutiny. For everything in the physical realm, there is a spiritual correlation. To soften the claim of a potential spiritual attack, you may hear something like, *I don't want to overspiritualize this*. But what does that mean? Either it is a spiritual attack or it's not.

On the other end of the spectrum, someone may claim a spiritual attack for their burnt toast that morning. The enemy is likely not paying that much attention to you when you're sitting on the couch eating burnt toast and watching Netflix, but when you start walking in obedience to God, that is when you are a threat to his agenda. Unless your toast had something to do with God's plan for His kingdom, likely the devil couldn't care less about it.

When you are walking in obedience to God's calling for His kingdom's work, that is when the enemy will step in and try to make things more difficult. When something unexpected happens, it will bring stress. In that moment, you can reflect on Philippians 4:6–7, which says,

> Do not be anxious about anything, but in everything by prayer and supplication with thanksgiving let your requests be made known to God. And the peace of God, which surpasses all understanding, will guard your hearts and your minds in Christ Jesus.

So when the enemy steps in and tries to throw a wrench in your plans, stop and pray, "Lord, you have called me to missions. I am walking in obedience to you, which threatens those who oppose you. I trust you to work in this situation and give me wisdom and strength to walk through it."

Now back to some practical details. Here are a few questions that need to be answered:

- Do you have an emergency contact both in the US (or your home country) as well as your future host country?
- Who is in charge of passports and tickets?
- Who is responsible for luggage?
- If you are traveling with children, will you need to provide birth certificates for your kids when you arrive in your host country?

Since I'm writing this amid the global COVID-19 pandemic:

- Is it required to provide negative virus tests to travel?
- Do you need to wear masks?
- Are vaccinations required?
- Do you need proof of immunization?
- Are there quarantine requirements?

First, let's talk about establishing emergency contacts. Having more than one emergency contact person (one in the country you are leaving and one in the country you are going to) will ensure that you will receive help if something happens. If authorities can reach the emergency contact who is geographically closer, you will likely get assistance a little faster. If you are three-quarters through your journey, it would be good to have someone closer who can respond to any emergencies that may come about.

Next, let's address passports. Your organization should know the requirements for visas and how many empty pages there should be in your passport for your future host country, but be sure that you know as well. For example, South Africa requires four blank pages in the back of your passport to enter the country. We had a friend and his family returning to the field, and he only had two empty pages in his passport, so he had to stay behind and get a new passport or added pages while his family went on without him. You can avoid that kind of stress if you know what's required or expected and take care of it before you get turned around at the airport.

Which brings us to tickets and luggage. Having one person keeping track of passports and tickets and the other in charge of luggage makes things run smoother and ensures you know where to place the blame if anything gets lost—kidding! The least amount of worry per person, the better. As you are checking in for your flight, the one handling passports and tickets can be at the counter, while the other ensures all the bags are with you. Or if you stop for a snack, you know that person will be keeping track of all the bags. Here's a friend's story on losing track of a bag:

> Finally, we had made it to the mid-way point of our trans-atlantic move to Africa. Having traveled to Germany previously, I had been dreaming for months about biting into a freshly baked, chewy pretzel. Things had gone well so far, I thought, congratulating myself on obsessively planning out every detail. We were almost to our hotel room on the other side of the airport, having taken a friend's advice to get some sleep on a long layover. It seemed quite a bit farther than anticipated with a thirteen-month-old, five-year-old,

and the maximum amount of allowed carry-on baggage, but the pretzel made it all worth it.

It seemed that our reservation was misplaced at the hotel, and we exceeded the capacity for the room we booked. We had to decide, while exhausted, if we wanted to pay three times as much for a suite. In the end, we paid, and the sleep was blissful. Eight hours later, upon checking out, we were horrified to discover that one of our suitcases was missing! I had left it at the pretzel stand. We ran there, and the lady was able to text her coworker and find out that the police had come to collect our bag. Unfortunately, lost and found was closed for the night, and we had to board our plane without it. The worst part was that my husband had put his irreplaceable flight log containing his pilot certifications in that suitcase so it would not get lost. Thankfully, many emails and three long months later, it caught up with us in Africa. That pretzel ended up being the most expensive one I have ever eaten. (K. Adams, personal communication June 5, 2021)

Our friends were so excited to get pretzels that they abandoned their assignments. Of course, let's remember this is a team effort. It is still good to be in communication with one another and help each other out.

So, what about birth certificates? Usually these are only required for children, but it is a good idea to have them for the adults as well. Investigate whether you will be required to provide birth certificates for your children upon entering your host country or any country you will travel through. For instance, with the increase in child trafficking around the globe, South Africa made it a requirement that everyone traveling with children provide original birth certificates for the children traveling with them. In addition, if one parent was traveling alone with the children, they also needed a police affidavit signed by the other parent stating they were authorized to travel with those children. They recently lifted those requirements, but it could go back into effect at any time.

Speaking of children, as I mentioned, I was pregnant during our travels, so I wanted to touch on that here. If you are or may become pregnant, ask yourself if you would be comfortable giving birth overseas or if you would want to return to America. So many people looked at me like I had three heads when I told them our child would be born in Africa. We were planning to deliver in South Africa, and their medical care is quite advanced. There were women on our program who had delivered their babies in South Africa, which put me at ease. It is certainly something to consider when commencing your adventures.

That brings us to viruses. Yuck. As I mentioned, I am writing this in 2021 amid the global COVID-19 pandemic. Currently, for South Africa, it is required that travelers be tested for the virus within seventy-two hours of travel and provide a negative test at the border. So whether it is COVID-19 or any other number of potential illnesses, it is a good idea to know the requirements for masks, testing, quarantines, or vaccinations as you make your travel arrangements.

It is also beneficial to know the currency exchange rates for the countries you will be passing through. For example, Bryan's mom passed through London when she came to visit us. She wanted to use cash for a bottle of water but only had US currency. The cashier took her five-dollar bill but gave no change. That was an expensive bottle of water! Lesson learned, use a card if you can, and know the exchange rates. I have an app on my phone called Currency Converter. It comes in handy when trying to figure out prices! You can get currency exchange rates for five different countries at once.

When your travel time spans more than forty hours, having these simple role assignments and details taken care of can take you from surviving to thriving by significantly reducing stress and increasing the enjoyment of your journey. If you also allow yourself extra transition time, as I will discuss next, you will have more capacity to deal with any unexpected events that may occur rather than stressing about what is next.

We're Best with Rest

The first leg of our forty-two-hour journey was about a ten-hour flight from Seattle to London. The flight was completely full, so there were no empty seats, making it difficult to sleep, especially for Bryan since he is so tall. When we landed, we had a seven-hour layover. That seems like a long time to be hanging out in an airport, but I believe it is best to allow as much time as possible for transitions when planning for a long journey. Since we didn't get much sleep on the plane, we found a couple of chairs and tried to rest. Being pregnant made that quite interesting, but we managed. As you can imagine, we didn't get the best sleep, but we closed our eyes. But we still had an eleven-hour flight to South Africa ahead of us!

As we boarded our flight from London to Johannesburg, we were exhausted. Though we got little cat-naps in those chairs, it was not enough. We were tired and stressed. I had swollen feet and hands and bags under my eyes. This flight was full as well. While there was an empty seat next to us and I could lie down using Bryan as a pillow, he could not stretch out at all. At this point, we just wanted to get there. There was little to no enjoyment of this next leg of our journey.

Fast-forward a few years: we discovered this wonderful invention called a hotel—in the airport! *Gasp!* Had we known what a difference it would make, we would have reserved a room for that layover time in London and gotten a shower and a proper rest. My suggestion to you is to make your layover time as restful as possible so you are fresh and able to enjoy the remainder of your journey. Though it may extend your total transit time, there is no shame in getting rest. Spending a little extra time and money to get a comfortable bed and shower is beneficial not just for you but also for those around you. Investing in a hotel room is well worth the money. Being more properly rested would have been amazing, especially during pregnancy. Hindsight is always twenty-twenty, right?

Some of you may feel a bit guilty about the idea of resting. You might want to just forge ahead. But let's take a minute to look at what God says about rest. After all, in your life as a missionary, you will constantly be attuned to others' needs and serving. But at the same time, you will need to learn to rest and sometimes take time for yourself. God rested on the seventh day after creating the universe, Jesus would often steal away for a respite to rest and pray, and Jesus told his disciples to rest. In Mark 6, the disciples were sent out in pairs, working long hours and traveling long distances. When they returned and reported to Jesus all they had been doing, Jesus told them, "'Come away by yourselves to a desolate place and rest a while.' For many were coming and going, and they had no leisure even to eat" (Mark 6:31 ESV). I can't stress it enough. There is absolutely no shame in scheduling rest. Are you traveling with children? They need rest, too, right?

It's also essential to hydrate! Everyone in your family should get water at every opportunity, as well as use the restroom. Dehydration can lead to water retention and added fatigue. You are allowed to carry an empty water bottle through security. So you can have one for each of you and fill it as needed. Our family has adopted the when-you-have-the-opportunity,-take-it mentality regarding using the bathroom and drinking water.

Let's think about food, entertainment, movement, and rest for the littles! If you are hoping your kids will sleep on the flight, it would be best to feed them before boarding the plane, as the meals may not arrive when you desire. On top of that, airplane food is not the most exciting or nutritious. In fact, when I went to Africa to visit Bryan, I had requested gluten-free meals. My meals were actually served frozen—all of them. Talk about disappointment! If you can plan for better food at the airport, maybe do a hard pass on the airline meal.

It would also be wise to have some entertainment suitable for your children. If they like to read, color, watch shows, or play games, bring their favorites on the plane. Extended layovers are amazing when traveling with kids! After being cooped up in a plane for ten-plus hours, they will need to move and, like you, to get proper rest! Research the airport(s) you will be going through to see what is available. Of course, most airports have restaurants and hotel rooms, but some even have play areas for kids.

My basic takeaway is that the better prepared you are going into your overseas journey, the less stressful and more enjoyable it will be. You know yourself. Bryan and I have discovered that we are the type who need to rest along the way. Others use their layover time to explore outside the airport. If you know exploring is something you could manage, by all means, explore. But if you're not sure, maybe save that for your next trip.

Special Companions

Touchdown Johannesburg! We made it! But wait, there's more! Wait! *What*?

We were fortunate that our journey to South Africa was pretty seamless, albeit tiring. Thankfully, we went through immigration, customs, and baggage claim in record time. Our teammate from Lesotho picked us up from the airport and took us out to breakfast. Finally, some real food—none of that airline junk. But we had more travel yet to come.

Not only was there a six-hour drive ahead of us, but we also had to stop to pick up Austin. Remember him, my naughty little husky? Yep, I couldn't bear the thought of leaving him with another family, so he had his own little international adventure. When we got to the kennel, we heard rave reviews on Austin's behavior and beauty. I was so pleased he did so well on his journey. The folks at the kennel were sad to see him go. He loaded up in the van no problem, and we headed to Lesotho.

If you can't bear the thought of leaving your furry family members behind and are thinking of bringing them with you, there are a few things to consider. First, check with your organization and your team in your future host country and see if it is allowed. Then check into the logistic side. Aside from the airline ticket costs (about the same as for humans) and international shipping and boarding, there are also tests, vaccinations, immigration paperwork, and USDA approval.

Some companies specialize in assisting with shipping your pet overseas. We had a company helping us on the South Africa side, so don't dismiss the idea entirely if it's important to you. Look into it and see if it is feasible for your family. For me, it was worth it. Looking back, I would do the same (for that dog). But we won't be shipping any animals overseas when the time comes again. The company we used was specific for South Africa, but the International Pet and Animal Transportation Association (IPATA) can help you find a pet shipping company for where you are going.

Knowing What's Ahead

Were you surprised when I mentioned that we had a six-hour drive ahead of us once we landed in South Africa? While the thought is exhausting, at least it was something we expected. That is something else to be aware of when you are planning your travels. Airline travel is taxing. It is good to know what is ahead once you arrive at your final destination. Is that truly your final destination, or is there more?

There are other things you should ask.

Who will be picking you up from the airport? If you haven't met them or talked with them, ask if they can send a picture and a phone number or other way to contact them.

Speaking of phones, you may want to start looking at unlocked SIM card phones. Most overseas phone plans are on SIM cards. I was able to find a dual SIM phone so that travel between South Africa and Lesotho would be easier. But it's not that difficult to swap out a SIM.

You can also ask:
- What will be waiting for you once you arrive at your new home?
- Will there be beds or other furniture?
- Will the beds be made up?
- Will there be groceries in your house or flat?
- Will someone be hosting you for dinner?

It would benefit you to ask these questions beforehand so you know how to prepare. If you are looking forward to sleeping in a nice warm bed, you would not be very pleased to find you will be using sleeping bags for a few days.

We were blessed to have our team move us into our home. They took all of Bryan's things out of storage and brought them to the house we would be living in. As a result, we had a bed and other comfortable furniture. Some of it was loaned to us temporarily, but we had places to sit, a table to eat at, and a place to sleep. Since your shipment likely won't arrive for a while (shipping times vary depending on the shipping company, destination, whether you're shipping air or sea freight, etc.), it would be good to know if your team has temporary furniture to use. Our sea shipment took about eight weeks to arrive (that was faster than most).

When we finally arrived in Lesotho, a family on our team hosted us for dinner. I'm sure the food was delicious, and they were terrific. But as friendly as they were, we were exhausted, and I don't remember much about that evening. They drove us home since neither of us was in any condition to drive. Not only because we were spent, but it had been over a year since Bryan had driven in Lesotho. And I had never driven in Lesotho or on the right side of the car or the left side of the road—ever—unless by accident!

We slept hard that night and woke up surprisingly refreshed the next day. Our teammates asked us how we were doing and if we were experiencing any jet lag. That is one of those things that seems to affect people in many different ways. We didn't experience much jet lag going to Africa, but a few years later, when we returned to the US on furlough, it hit us pretty hard. However, we have a friend who is exactly the opposite—she's fine going to America, but terrible going back to Africa. I suppose you will find out which camp you are in once you travel.

Either direction you go, there are many theories out there. I have heard that it takes about one day to adjust for each time zone you cross. We crossed ten so theoretically, it would take about ten days to adjust, which was pretty accurate when we traveled to the US. Most people will take at least a few days to adjust to their new time zone. Be sure to keep that in mind as you plan your excursions in your new country.

No Fear

It is up to your husband and you to lead your family into the land God has called you for this time. Do not fear. The Lord will be with you. After the death of Moses, it was up to Joshua to lead the Israelites into the Promised Land. The Lord said to Joshua, "Have I not commanded you? Be strong and courageous. Do not be frightened, and do not be dismayed, for *the Lord your God is with you wherever you go*" (Joshua 1:9).

As with most things, our fears typically find their roots in the unknown. If you have concerns about traveling internationally, rest assured that it can be a wonderful experience the more you prepare. Draw on the experiences of those who have walked the path before you. With a plan and some research beforehand, your travel can be seamless, allowing you to focus on your family and navigate any unforeseen circumstances that may arise.

Reflection:

Think about traveling internationally.

- What fears do you have?
- What do you still need to do to get the practical details of travel taken care of?

Think about your planning strategy for travel.

- Who is responsible for passports, tickets, and baggage?
- What have you discovered about the airports you will be traveling through?

Think about your personality regarding travel.

- What are your plans for layovers?
- Are you one to rest or explore?

Think about any special circumstances surrounding your travel.

- Are you traveling with children?
- What are your plans for their food, entertainment, exercise, and rest?
- What are your plans if you are shipping a pet?

I invite you to pray with me.

Prayer:

Father God, I confess my fear of the unknown and my fears of something happening as we travel. Lord, I lay those fears down at your feet. I choose to walk in obedience to your calling on my life. I pray for your protection against any attacks that may come upon my family. I pray that I may plan to the best of my ability, covering the practical aspects of travel to equip myself to handle the spiritual aspects. Thank you for your grace and mercy upon us as we travel. I pray in Jesus's name, amen.

CHAPTER 8

Settling In

*Having our roots firmly established in Christ enables us to make
our home anywhere.*

I LINGERED IN BED A LITTLE longer than usual, even though I woke up refreshed and ready for the day! I listened to the new sounds that would become so familiar over the next few years. The birds' songs were in harmony as they danced through the trees in our yard. Once I was up and showered, I poured a cup of coffee and stepped outside. I breathed in the crisp fall air and watched Austin chase the birds in the yard. (Wait, fall? Didn't you arrive in May? Yep, seasons are opposite in the southern hemisphere.)

It was my first wake up living in Lesotho, Africa, and Bryan and I decided to go into town. Guess who drove—I did! My first day and I was already driving! Not only that, but I was driving a large van with a manual transmission with the gear shift on the left. It was like driving with my dad again, except I was pushing the pedals and steering too! I did great, considering the steering wheel was on the right side of the car, and I was driving on the left side of the road.

Overall, it was a good day. I felt like a rock star! We explored enough to get my bearings and figure out how to get home. We did a little shopping to get some essentials for our home, then got some lunch. Then the fatigue set in, so we called it a day. I guess the jet-lag bug had caught us after all.

Jumping In

Many people fear the unknown of exploring in a foreign country. Driving, shopping, communicating—they are all scary! However, it takes time to get used to shopping in any new place—even switching grocery stores in America—so that is nothing to fear. One thing that may help, especially if you're exploring when you're tired, is to bring your camera into the store or marketplace and take pictures of familiar things—or foreign things that somehow got your attention. You can take photos of the aisles to remember where you saw something, so it is not so foreign the next time you return. If you are really ambitious, you could even take a video as you shop! GoPro anyone? Too much?

Communication is always tricky. I have been fortunate to live in a country where English is a primary trade language. However, you may very well be trying to negotiate a foreign language on top of all the other cultural adjustments you have to make. If your foreign language training is in your host country, your language helper might also assist you in navigating the culture. If you studied in language school before arriving in your host country, it would be wise to ask if there is a language or cultural guide to help you for the first few months in the country.

Maybe you are petrified of driving overseas. I know some people who don't like driving at all, let alone in a foreign country. Or perhaps shopping is a challenge for you, and the thought of navigating a new culture and new shopping experiences makes you cringe. Or if you are an introvert like me, the idea of practicing your language skills with strangers is paralyzing! These fears are normal, but don't let your fear stop you from thriving in your new culture. Just jump in!

As much as it terrified me to drive in a foreign country, I did not want to be paralyzed by fear. I knew the longer I waited, the harder it would be. Jumping in is usually the best way to adjust to a new culture. Typically, other than the fear of crashing a vehicle, the fear that grips us is the fear of looking or feeling foolish when we make mistakes. But do you laugh at a child who falls when he is learning to walk? Do you laugh at a new Christian for asking questions about the Bible? Do you laugh at someone from another country when she makes a mistake using English? Of course not, nor should you fear others will laugh at you when you make mistakes with language or cultural differences. On the contrary, those in host cultures are usually impressed that you are attempting to use their language and learn their culture.

In any new culture, it is of utmost importance that you engage the culture with respect and reverence as Paul did in Athens, as described in Acts 17. Paul took note of all the idols to other gods throughout the city, but he did not condemn them for it. He observed and took notice of one idol erected and inscribed with "To the unknown god." Paul taught them that was the altar for the one true God. He did not mock or scold them for their worship practices. Instead, he was respectful of their culture and religion and preached the truth in love as we are to do.

Sweet Sanctuary

One missionary spouse I spoke with told me she struggled with creating a peaceful home once she moved overseas. She wanted to create a sanctuary, a place for her family to retreat after navigating a foreign culture all day. This particular family moved into a house her organization had been renting for more than twenty years! Many different families had occupied it, so of course, it had the characteristics of those families within its walls.

There is a sense of home that everyone knows. Though not everyone feels it when they go to the house they live in, they still know the feeling—and notice its absence. So many long for it—many more even strive for it. That familiarity is what brings a sigh of relief, knowing that you can relax in your own environment, set up just the way you like, with your own furniture. And while there may be things that still need fixing, the comfort of home is still there.

No matter where you live, it is important to have a place for daily respite. It feels even more essential living in a foreign country. When you join a missions organization, you may not have much say in where you live, as housing choices overseas are often few and far between. Of course, it depends on the development of the country you are going to, but where we live, the construction is not the quality we were used to in America. Most missionaries face one common reality: they likely have quite a bit of work ahead of them. But please remember that a house does not define home, and there is no one-size-fits-all method of establishing a home.

So what does it mean to make a home? Well, that is different for everyone. When faced with the aspect of setting up home in a rental house overseas, let's use the old lemon cliché: "When life gives you lemons, make lemonade." Some people turn lemons into lemonade, and others choose to make a lemon meringue pie! Then there are others who just opt for sliced lemons. How will you use your lemons?

Setting Up Home

When we first arrived at our rental house in Lesotho, we had barely parked the car—in front of the garage—before a list of potential home improvements began to form itself in my mind. *I wonder if we should make the garage operational.* As we walked up the walkway, I narrowly avoided tripping into a foot-wide runoff ditch. *I wonder if we should put a grate over that.* Navigating along the narrow curved pathway to the entry. *I wonder if we should widen this walkway so the stroller will fit.* As we entered the house, more renovation ideas floated through my head. *We may need to redo this floor. This wall needs paint—what should we do about that big crack that runs from the ceiling to the floor? I'd love to paint the baby's room.*

Individual families are responsible for the upkeep of the houses our organization rents for our team. Minor upgrades are usually no problem, and we can make significant upgrades with the landlord's approval. Sometimes they will even pay for them. However, this can come at a higher cost than just materials and labor. For example, I heard a story of a family who made beautiful upgrades to the home they were renting. Sadly, the landlord stopped by to check on something and loved what they had done so much that he decided he could get more rent! Thus, that family moved because they couldn't afford what the landlord now wanted them to pay.

After hearing that story, I was a little cautious of making any upgrades to our house. So when we arrived, we adopted the make-the-most-of-what-you-have mentality. We didn't just settle for sliced lemons, but we sure weren't shooting for lemon meringue pie! Of all the enhancements we thought about making to that house, only one made the must-have list: a new floor. Of the list of minor changes, only one made the top: Painting the baby's room. The rest came as the years ticked on. We did what we could to make our house comfortable.

Five months pregnant and stir crazy, I entered into that oft-talked-about "nesting phase" of pregnancy. Just painting the walls was not enough. I wanted a tree on the wall of the nursery. So I dug deep within myself and found a long-dormant talent for art, and I decided to draw a tree. But I didn't stop there. I drew monkeys, elephants, and giraffes too—each one a mom with a baby. Then, with the help of some ladies on the team, I painted the safari grass and sky. It was a beautiful mural that spanned three of the four walls of our baby's room. The only reason it wasn't on the fourth was that it was the closet!

Maybe you are like me, and you have ideas for creating beauty but have lower standards for comfort. I am a jeans-and-sweatshirt comfort kind of gal. If I have a couch and a blanket, a few knick-knacks decorating the shelves, and my family photos on the wall, I'm happy. Or maybe you need a little bit more—perhaps you like matching furniture and pretty table settings and matching lamps. That's fair. I like pretty things too. Comfort requirements even differ between spouses. Bryan was in more of a take-what-we-get mentality, while I wanted to add a little more comfort. But over the years, he came to realize that since I spent my whole day in the house, spending a little extra money or putting in a little extra work was worth it for my comfort.

There is no right or wrong for wherever you fall on the spectrum. Just know that going overseas may mean dealing with significant imperfections in the construction, peeling paint, ugly stucco, or dilapidated outbuildings. You can decide now how much work you are willing to put in or wait until you see what you have to work with. But I'm sharing this chapter as a means to be prepared.

Settling for Good Enough

After putting in all that work on our house, we stayed there for three and a half years and then went on our six-month home assignment in America. We returned to Lesotho with our now three-and-a-half-year-old son (and I was once again five months pregnant during our overseas travel). There were fewer families on our team, and the house we were living in was the most expensive, so they asked us to move. So one month after returning to Africa, we were fixing up another place to make it livable.

Once again, I found myself nesting by painting and cleaning, but this time I had even more help from our team and the community we had built in our first three years. Though we weren't surprised by the request to move (we knew that it would likely happen), it did pain me to let go of the hard work I'd put into my kids' rooms in the other house. It was a painful reminder that our home is in our hearts, not on our walls.

I had attempted to put down roots in a temporary, earthly house—that we were only renting. I needed to be reminded that my roots are in Christ, not in a house. Paul said, "Therefore, as you received Christ Jesus the Lord, so walk in him, *rooted and built up in Him* and established in the faith, just as you were taught, abounding in thanksgiving" (Colossians 2:6–7). Having our roots firmly established in Christ enables us to make our home anywhere.

We chose not to do too much elaborate decorating in this house. However, I did paint some accent walls, hung some pictures and lovely black-out curtains, and put up some shelves for my knick-knacks. In addition, we took out the old dirty carpet and replaced it with laminate flooring, which was a lot of work but made it comfortable for us. After our first housing experience, I decided that putting in a ton of work on a house we had to leave was not crucial for my comfort. So while we strive to leave the places we use in better condition than how we found them, we've chosen to leave the significant upgrades for those who deem it more valuable.

Living cross-culturally can be draining, so it is essential to have a comfortable home where you can unwind, a safe place to process, where you can be yourself and relax with your family without wondering how it will influence those around you. Yes, it is appropriate to make your house functional, comfortable, and even beautiful to suit you and your needs. However, much like how we pare down our belongings knowing they are temporary, we need to view our housing as temporal as well.

When a new family joined our team (the wife has since become a dear friend of mine), much work went into finding a suitable house for them. I have to say, when we saw the house, most of the expats—a term used for one living outside their passport country—were all a bit perplexed. When my friend arrived, I am pretty sure she cried. The layout of the house was weird—for lack of a better word. The house was essentially one big hallway, and the driveway was pretty much impossible to navigate without a 4x4 with high clearance.

She made that house as comfortable as she possibly could. I loved what she did with what she had. On top of super-cute decor, she set up a quaint little coffee area with a high table and bar stools and a lovely sitting area. She made the best of the situation. I am not that creative. Had we gotten that house, after a few hours of crying, I probably would have requested a different one as soon as humanly possible. I still wonder how she did it. I would say she is a lemon-meringue gal! In comparison, I suppose that would make me more of a sour lemonade gal.

How you go about setting up your home will be different depending on where you end up in the world. I can only speak for where I've served, so if you are in contact with someone in your future host country, you can ask them if upgrades will be necessary or allowed and if the landlord covers the cost, etc. If you have items you feel are essential to make your house a home, bring them along. While there may not be a Target or a Bed, Bath & Beyond, there will likely be home decorating outlets or even local vendors where you can purchase items that will add beauty and comfort, and some may even bring in the feel of your host culture.

Culture Shock

I was thankful to be doing my home decorating during our first few months in Lesotho. Things seemed to become more difficult as the months went on and the effects of culture shock set in. When I woke up to the singing and dancing birds our first morning in Lesotho, I was excited for what was ahead. I wanted to jump into the culture, make new friends, and establish my routine. Much like the first few months of marriage, life was amazing, and I loved everything about our new country. I was in the honeymoon stage of our overseas journey.

Our organization taught us about the four phases of culture shock: the honeymoon phase, the frustration phase, the adjustment phase, and the acceptance phase. I have certainly gone through all these stages, and it seems they behave much like the stages of grief. There is no distinct transition from one to the next, and they seem to ebb and flow between phases. The shift is different for everyone, and often it will catch you off guard.

By the time I had been in Lesotho for about five months, my excitement began to plummet, signaling a downward slope into the frustration phase. I was almost eight months pregnant. I hadn't had many cravings for sweets during my pregnancy, but one day we were out shopping, and I just wanted some ice cream. So Bryan and I stopped at a fast-food restaurant and requested an ice cream cone. The clerk flashed us a friendly grin and playfully asked who it was for. I played back, pointed at my belly, and said, "This guy." She snickered a little and then said, "No, I can't serve you ice cream." Thinking she was trying to pull a fast one on the white lady, I started laughing and expected her to start laughing and turn around to get my ice cream. But she was serious. I stood in disbelief. She flat-out refused to serve me ice cream because I was pregnant, and her manager backed her up.

Ministering to people in a culture different from my own was challenging for my heart. While I wanted to love them and share about Jesus, I often found myself aching that I couldn't change how the people did things. I feared that people would see my frustration before they would see Jesus. For example, when I worked at the orphanage, the children who needed the most attention were often neglected and left in a corner. The little time I would get with them once or twice a week was not enough. They needed more consistent care, but there were not enough volunteers, and there was no physiotherapist in the country who could see them more than once a month. It broke my heart that I couldn't implement a change that would last.

That I still talk about my ice cream experience with such vivid memory and frustration tells me that this phase of culture shock seeps into all aspects of life overseas. While I can laugh about it now, there's still a hint of bitterness. Refusing to serve ice cream to a pregnant woman should be grounds for some sort of lawsuit. And a culture that believes a pregnant woman shouldn't eat ice cream can't be trusted, right? The frustrations that you have during this time will stick with you for a while, though when you enter into the subsequent phases, they won't have as much of an effect on you, and you may even be able to laugh about them.

It probably took about a year before I began the upward shift into the adjustment phase. Bryan and I were out at a restaurant for a date night. Although it was a higher-end place, I was sure to select three items because by this time I knew that just because the item was on the menu, it did not mean that it was available. Sure enough, they did not have my first or second choice. I shook my head and laughed as the server apologized. I have to chuckle a little bit at this memory because, though we wouldn't have seen it then, I see it now. While it was inconvenient, I *expected* them not to have what I wanted, so it was easier to accept, whereas a few months earlier I might have had a less composed reaction.

Asking if menu items were available before getting my hopes up indicated that I was moving up the culture shock curve. In addition, minor things weren't bothering me as much anymore, like taxis stopping short in front of me and long lines at the water company. And I came to expect pedestrians to step in front of my car without looking. While I was not too fond of these practices, at least I wasn't getting angry or frustrated. These things indicated that I had entered into the acceptance phase.

We experience culture shock in part because our host cultures don't think like us, act like us, or even understand the world as we do. Though I would not say that everything in America is done right, it's done the way I expect it to be. For example, if I buy something in America and it's not quite what I wanted, I can take it back to the store and exchange it or get my money back, no questions asked. But if I want to return something I purchased in Lesotho, it would take about an hour or more to get all the manager's signatures and written explanations of why we were returning the product. And after that, if we had opened the package, they would not take it back anyway. Coming from a culture that prides itself on efficiency, that it could take two hours at the store to get a refund—or be denied a refund—can be infuriating.

While not all culture shock experiences will be the same, you will notice a pattern in your journey. You may find that everything seems to be more difficult in a foreign culture, from shopping to cleaning. It seems to take more effort, because it's not what we are used to. We have to figure out minor things like where to get a haircut and more significant things like where to go for a medical emergency. But once you get through all the phases, it becomes easier to navigate the culture, and you may even come to enjoy the little quirks that used to bother you. You may not get back to your initial feelings, but you will begin to feel comfortable and at home.

Once I learned to expect things to take longer than they should, that I probably wouldn't be able to return something, or that the taxi drivers and pedestrians would not change their ways—no matter how violently I shook my fist at them—then I was able to start embracing the culture a bit more. This shift also helped in my orphanage ministry. Being in a different mindset enabled me to focus on what I *could* do rather than what I couldn't. Not expecting the government to change its ways freed me to share the love of Jesus through ministering to the children who needed my help.

Not of This World

If you recall, back in high school, I was always the new girl. At one school I attended, most students had grown up together and had known one another since grade school. I had no idea what that was like, and frankly, I didn't care to know. That wasn't who I was, and I would never fit in with them. I felt like I was on the outside of all these little cliques of girls, but by then, I had grown comfortable with my inability to fit in.

That seemingly unacceptable trait became a tool God used for revelation during my time overseas. Fitting in is not a goal of mine, and living overseas in a culture different from my own is no exception. "If the world hates you, know that it has hated me before it hated you. If you were of the world, the world would love you as its own; but because *you are not of the world*, but I chose you out of the world, therefore the world hates you" (John 15:18–19).

When I say we can "embrace the culture," I mean we can accept and appreciate the people in our host country for who they are and how they do things. I am not talking about assimilating, as in trying to become one of them. Rather, we needed to adapt and alter our expectations and adjust how we see the world to live among and understand the culture of our host country. As I discussed earlier, we should not give up who we are to fit into any culture, but we should be adaptable enough to live among them.

The apostle Paul said, "I have become all things to all people, that by all means I might save some. I do it all for the sake of the gospel, that I may share with them in its blessings" (1 Corinthians 9:22–23). While he became "all things to all people," he did not conform to their way of life. But he sought to understand them, be among them, and be like them to better communicate the gospel of Christ. As Christians, we are missionaries no matter what continent we are on or what job we do.

Bryan and I found ourselves in a unique position to offer premarital counseling to some national friends. Counseling, in general, is not popular in Lesotho, let alone premarital counseling. However, extramarital affairs are common and widely accepted. Our friends did not want to fall prey to cultural acceptances, so it was a blessing to walk with them as they prepared for their marriage, not just a wedding. Our counsel went against the grain of the culture to ensure that our friends held Christ at the center of their marriage. We didn't fit in with the culture, and though our friends were raised in that culture, they didn't fit in either—because they were Christians.

As Christians, we are not of this world, and thus we should not conform to the standards of this world and have them shape us, but we are to be shaped by Christ. In essence, not fitting in is a good thing, and we should embrace it. No foreign missionary will ever truly fit in with the people of their host country. And after being in our host country for a while, I began to feel I would never fit in with my home culture anymore either. I think this is right where God wants us to be, in the in-between. We are rooted in Christ.

Reflection:
Think about the culture you will be living in.
- What fears do you have about the culture?
- What will you need to encourage yourself to jump in and explore?

Think about setting up a home.
- When you think about establishing a home in your host country, what is your main goal?
- Are you aiming to provide a peaceful sanctuary you and your family can come home to?
- Is your goal to impress others or to be comfortable?

Think about how different your future host culture will be from your home culture.
- How does it help you prepare yourself in knowing that culture shock is something that happens to everyone?
- In an earlier chapter I talked about being rooted in Christ. How does that affect your desire to fit in to a society?
- How did you feel when I said you would not fit in anywhere?

Think about how you might feel being a minority in a foreign culture.
- Is your desire to be accepted for who you are or to fit in with those around you?
- What do you need to put in place to remind yourself that although you don't fit in, God has you right where He wants you?

I invite you to pray with me.

Prayer:
Father God, I pray you would prepare my heart for the challenges that come with living overseas. Prepare my mind for the potential aesthetic differences I will face when making a rental home comfortable for my family and me. Please bring the resources I will need to create a sanctuary and fill our home with your peace. I pray for contentment with the available furnishings and that it wouldn't matter what my furniture looks like. I also pray I would stay rooted in you, knowing I am not of this world, and I could minister to those in this new culture without the need to fit in.

CHAPTER 9

Living Life with Others

*There is no way to prepare for the curve balls life may throw at us.
Having others to walk beside us and help field them is beyond
priceless.*

"I WANT TO GO HOME!" THE words tumbled right out, along with the tears mixed with sweat streaming down my face. I wanted to take them back before I even finished the sentence. How would going back to America make any of this easier? "We are home." I immediately corrected myself and buried my face into Bryan's chest, soaking his shirt with my tears. It was less than a week before Christmas. We stood in the midmorning heat, drenched with sweat but still clinging to one another in the doorway. After everything we had been through with the chaos of planning for the baby, problems with our car, delivering the baby, and compounded medical issues, to say we were dumbfounded at what was happening would be an understatement.

Since we had arrived in Lesotho, we had been constantly on the go. Despite my claims of being stir crazy, there was plenty for me to take care of. It seemed like every time I turned around, I would find something else to do. I was like a whirling dervish. Find a birthing clinic—check, spin; find a midwife—check, spin; find a doctor—check, spin. You get the idea. It seemed as if there was always something to be done. We needed to find a place to stay for a month, buy a car, make friends, be good teammates, unpack, and furnish our home—to name a few.

Our birthing clinic was in Johannesburg. Since it was a six-hour drive for our doctor appointments, we purchased a car for the long trips instead of borrowing one from our program. Unfortunately, our first trip to Johannesburg in our new-to-us Land Rover found us broken down outside a shopping mall with a completely fried transmission. Thankfully, a family from our team just happened to be staying at the same missions hostel that weekend, and once the mechanic got our car in a workable condition, our friends followed us back to Lesotho.

Regrettably, our Land Rover never made it back to the land of the living—maybe it stayed in the land of the roving? So we went back to borrowing a tiny car from our program. It was a tight fit with a month's worth of luggage plus baby stuff. The car seat was wedged against the front seat even with it all the way forward—leaving pregnant ol' me with absolutely no leg room. *I'm so glad the baby would be able to stretch out.*

We had arranged accommodation with a couple in Johannesburg through a missionary friend in Lesotho. They said we could stay for however long we needed. When we arrived at their home, I could hardly believe this was true. Their luxurious home was stunning and had plenty of space for us and quite a few others. Our host apologized that it wasn't more comfortable, and my face blushed. *What could she mean? This is perfect!* She invited us to make ourselves at home and showed us the key to the main house, and also invited us to share dinners throughout our stay. This family was a true blessing from God.

During our stay, we met another missionary from Lesotho who also stayed with our host family. We told him our Land Rover story, and he jokingly admonished us for buying a Land Rover, laughing that he drove one as well. It just so happened that he had a car for sale—not a Land Rover. So we exchanged contact information and planned to meet up when we returned.

We'd been living in Lesotho for five months and had been in South Africa for two weeks when our son was born perfectly healthy via an emergency C-section. Our host family's daughter was the first to visit us at the clinic. After continually battling infections the last few months of my pregnancy, we were thankful to have a healthy baby. Once the doctor determined we were healthy enough to travel, we headed home to Lesotho. Unfortunately, infections continued to plague my body, and two of them had to be taken care of surgically, the first in November and the second in December.

When Bryan and I stood baking in the doorway that day in December, we had just returned home from my second surgery the day before. When we entered the house, my stomach somersaulted with the stench wafting through the air. The hair on my arms stood on end as I slowly tiptoed through the debris that covered the floor. Every cabinet in the kitchen was open. A chair our friend had presumably used to hold a cabinet closed lay toppled on its side. It looked as if our home had been burglarized, but there were empty food packages and other garbage scattered throughout the house. We also found piles of feces in nearly every corner of the house, even on the couch—scratch the burglary theory.

In the three hours that had passed between our friend checking on him and us arriving home, our dog, Austin, had opened every cabinet, and either before or after rummaging through the garbage, devoured a whole ten-pound bag of chocolate chips! Knowing chocolate is toxic to dogs, we had intentionally stored them in a cabinet with a flush door, so how he got to them remains a mystery. But obviously, even at ten years old, he had not outgrown his naughtiness.

Since I was not supposed to lift anything, Bryan got our two-month-old down for a rest. I tried to get some rest as well while Bryan rushed Austin to the vet. Unfortunately, the vet misdiagnosed him as having tick-bite fever—a prevalent animal killer in Lesotho—even though Bryan told him what had happened. Bryan brought Austin home, and we tried to nurse him back to health overnight, but it was too late. The toxicity had coursed through his entire body. Considering my condition, I held him as best I could as he breathed his last. My naughty dog had given a literal meaning to the phrase "death by chocolate."

Calling on Community

When I arrived in Lesotho, I knew only one family on our team, Justin and Amanda, a married couple whose early journey looked a lot like ours. I only knew them because Bryan was friends with them before we got married—and Amanda was very instrumental in helping our relationship move forward. Of course I had met the rest of the team, but I hadn't developed those relationships yet. For the first few years, I didn't have much of a community outside our team.

My relationship with Amanda had grown in that short but challenging seven months I'd been in Lesotho. The morning after Austin died, she and another friend from our Bible study brought a breakfast casserole, crispy bacon, freshly baked biscuits, and flowers already in a vase. She didn't ask if she could come, she just told me she was coming. She knew she had that freedom with me. She didn't ask what I needed. She knew I didn't have an answer. So she just provided what she thought might be helpful.

The breakfast was lovely, and it was a relief not having to cook. But the most beautiful thing she offered me that day was empathy. She had no idea what was going on in my heart, but she sat with me. She had no idea how much pain I was feeling physically or emotionally, nor could she imagine it, but she knew I was hurting, and she cried with me. The greatest gift she gave me that day was the gift of her presence.

Our community showed up for us in so many ways; we know that we would have been lost without them. People we didn't even have a personal relationship with stepped up to help us. Through our community, we had a place to stay while we waited for our son to be born, where we were introduced to someone who had a car for sale—who also got us to the doctor when I needed to have my first surgery. We had someone to take care of our home and dog while we were away, and our community took care of us when things were so difficult I didn't want to get out of bed, let alone get a meal on the table.

There is no way to prepare for the curveballs life may throw at us, but having someone to walk beside us and help field them is beyond priceless. The perception of community is different for everyone, much like what we each need to be comfortable in our homes. How much we value or desire community will likely shine through when we find ourselves floundering like a fish out of water in our new environment, desperate for some semblance of familiarity.

As Americans, most of us have a sense of independence and individuality that pushes out the necessity or want for community, even in church. Even though we stress the importance of doing life with others and encourage being part of a small group and church community, it seems to be more about combating loneliness than encouraging community outside Sunday church sermons. We may not see those people more than twice a week. Yes, yes, I know there are exceptions, and many people have their close-knit friends. I have friends in America that I would call family. But what would it be like to have deeper relationships and call on them and rely on them for things? *Hey Jenn, I'm having a rough day; I could use some company. Could you come over?*

Our pride tells us we can do everything on our own, and we don't need anyone else, which in a sense is true. There are plenty of competent people in the country who manage considerably well on their own. But God's word tells us, "Two are better than one, because they have a good reward for their toil. For if they fall, one will lift up his fellow. But woe to him who is alone when he falls and has not another to lift him up!" (Ecclesiastes 4:9–10). We are a take-care-of-myself society, and many who do fall, fall alone.

Moving overseas takes that independent confidence and dumps it on its prideful head. Instead of calling a friend or neighbor when we are having a bad day, we might veg out in front of a screen or do something else to occupy our mind so we don't have to think about the pain.

When we realize we don't have eggs, we'd likely load up the kids and go to the store. When you move overseas, you may discover that the one store available to buy groceries is out of eggs most days of the week, and you either need to shop on the day they stock the shelves or find a local poulterer to buy eggs from. How do you make such discoveries? Many are through trial and error, but most come from the community surrounding you.

Your Team Is Your Family

Your team may often be your only source of community, whether you like them or not. Understandably, the people on your team may not be those you would typically choose to be friends with, so it becomes time to look at them as family. You didn't choose the family you were born into, but they are still family and will likely be there for you when you need them. Such is the case for team members. Whether you choose them or not, or whether you like them or not, they will ensure you are cared for.

Amanda knew me better than most of the people on our team. Building our relationship took work—more work for her—but it was something we both needed. So she put up with me and all my mess, and we became good friends. When she came with breakfast and comforted me after my dog died, she knew I just needed someone beside me. She was Jesus with skin on in that moment.

Bryan's community seems somewhat built in. He has guys and gals to communicate with daily at work. He can walk across the hangar and have a quick chat with a coworker pretty much anytime, whereas I have to venture out to find community, which likely includes driving across town just to have a conversation. I would become acquainted with others through attending social events: a Bible study, crafting group, or another engagement someone might have heard about. Hearing things through the grapevine was often the source of opportunities to socialize with other women.

Once I did hear about something, if I wanted to attend, it wasn't like walking across the hangar or down the street. Often it required driving across town. I wasn't afraid of driving, but I dreaded facing traffic more than once or twice a week. So I would offer to host so that I would not have to drive anywhere. If someone else was hosting, I would schedule shopping around that time, so I wouldn't have to go out again that week. And if it was planned during heavy traffic hours,

I would pass. My obsessive need for efficiency manifested tenfold once I moved overseas.

Things got more complicated if I met someone I wanted to spend more time with. We would have to schedule in a "coffee/play-date," and one of us would have to pack up our kid(s) and head out of the house for an afternoon of girl talk. That may not seem like a big deal, and it may be what you are already doing to make time with your girlfriends, but as I've mentioned, everything seems more difficult overseas. Of course, this is less of an issue if your team lives on a compound, but our team does not.

Take a moment to think about where you are going or might be going. What might your community look like? Will you be serving with an organization that has a team in your new host culture? Do you know anyone on that team? I wonder if you could email some of them or form a message group to start building your community before you go?

Maybe you are an introvert, and the thought of meeting up with people sounds exhausting and overwhelming. As an introvert myself, I find it overwhelming at times. Maybe after you meet up with people, it takes a couple of days to find your peace again. But let me tell you if you don't already know: when you go through a rough time, you will be thankful to have those people to call on, and they will be thankful to have you to call on as well.

Expat Community

I am not trying to scare you and say that building community is impossible. It's not. But two things I want to clarify: It is more challenging to build a community overseas, and it is essential to build a community overseas. There are ways to make it work. Perhaps you take turns hosting a small group or Bible study each week so that one of you gets a break from having to drive once in a while. Maybe you carpool and take turns driving so that you aren't always alone in the car, and you also get a break from driving now and again. However you choose to make it happen, you will benefit greatly from having a group of people you can call when you need something.

Consider expanding your community with expats outside of your team. Remember that not all of your friends need to be in Christian circles. If you see someone in the grocery store who looks like you, don't be afraid to say hello and introduce yourself. You can ask about them and what they are doing there and maybe even exchange contact information. Of course, not every expat you meet will be living there full time (we have Peace Corps volunteers passing through quite a bit), but it never hurts to say hello. You may even make their day.

There are benefits to having friends outside your built-in community. Some expats, perhaps those working in positions other than missions, may stay longer in their host country, so you may get to have a friend in the country longer. You might have things you do not feel comfortable sharing with people on your team. When you need to talk it out, it is a beautiful gift to have someone outside your team to voice your struggles to. You could also have a counselor on standby for that. In general, it's a good idea to develop a more diverse community.

Having others who are like minded to do life with becomes a much bigger deal when living cross-culturally. If only to have someone who gets it. Someone to sit and nod her head while you voice your frustrations about traffic circles and taxi drivers. Someone to empathize because they also purchased spoiled milk earlier that week. Someone to vent to about your house-helper misplacing the spoons again. To be heard and understood is a valuable gift when living in a culture you don't fully understand.

National Community

While building an expat community is important, it is equally important to have a community of nationals, a term used for the citizens of your host country. National friends can help you navigate the culture, introduce you to other people, show you some hole-in-the-wall places to get great food, or even show you a market to get a better value on produce.

Having friends in my host culture has helped me view things from a different perspective. Earlier I mentioned how my obsessive need for efficiency had manifested tenfold. Well, the people of Lesotho are more people-oriented than task-oriented. They value *relationships* over efficiency. My national friends have helped me understand that it is disrespectful not to address others before jumping into work. Saying good morning before asking for something and saying goodbye at the day's end are essential to maintaining healthy, respectful relationships. They have also helped me understand some of the things that irritate me—like taxi drivers. I get it. They're just trying to get a fare to make some money; they have families too. However, that does not make me feel any better when they stop short in front of me. I discovered most of our national friends share my taxi-driver terror!

Our national friends also help us navigate and understand the political culture. For example, when we had been in Lesotho for just over a year, there was an attempted political coup. When the police stopped patrolling and there was an increase in crime, the nationals on our staff helped us understand the news broadcast and the danger level, which helped us decide to evacuate to South Africa.

It's also beneficial to have a friend to call if you have a fender-bender. Emergencies and traffic incidents are handled quite differently overseas than in America. If you have an accident in Lesotho, you are required to leave your vehicle right where it is until the police come to investigate. Sometimes it can take hours for the police to arrive. The same rules apply for a bike vs. car incident! Bryan was riding his bike one day with a national friend and a teammate who is friends with a police officer, and a taxi driver—*grrr*—pulled out in front of him. Bryan couldn't stop in time, so he ran into the car, leaving a dent in the fender from his front wheel. Fortunately, no one was injured, but they all had to stay where they were until the police came to investigate. Since they had friends to call on, the police handled things fairly quickly, and thankfully, the police agreed that Bryan was in the right and the taxi driver was deemed at fault. Yay for small victories!

I touch on the benefits of national relationships for those who may shy away from developing cross-cultural relationships. Since you are going into missions, that may seem counterintuitive. But there is a difference between developing ministry relationships and developing friendships. For instance, you will have a relationship with those you minister to different from those you minister with. So while you will have relationships with those you minister to, it's not the same as having a friendship with them.

Think of it as a counselor-patient relationship. A counselor is not going to share his problems with his patient as he would with a friend. Here I am talking about seeking friendship for the sake of friendship alone without the goal of ministry—though often opportunities to share the gospel are a side benefit. Those friends Bryan rides with are a perfect example. They are just riding buddies. But because Bryan loves Christ, that love pours out of him into those guys he rides with. They may just be riding through the mountains together, but they are being ministered to just by being around Bryan.

Outside Ministry
Ministry outside your home is another way to develop relationships. I started providing manual therapy to the children at the orphanage after I had been in Lesotho for about two months. I became good friends with the directors and some of the volunteers. Shortly after I began, I came down with an infection, so I needed to stop. Once our son was about six months old, I felt well enough to go back. I would take him with me, and my friend, the director, would watch him for me while I ministered to the kids there. My time was mutually rewarding as I ministered to the children and continued to develop lasting friendships with the volunteers that would come through. When I look back, though, I wish I had waited to start until we had been in the country for at least six months.

If you are wondering when to begin ministry outside the home, based on my experience, I would recommend waiting six months unless, of course, you have a job that you are contracted to do. Waiting allows you to get settled in a bit and at least go through one or two phases of culture shock, which we discussed earlier. It is more difficult to enjoy your ministry when you are in the downward spiral of frustration. Once you move into the adaptation phase, minister on!

Kids in Community

All this talk about community for mom and dad, what about the littles? They need friends too! Well, what about school? School is touted as the best way to socialize kids even in America. Every homeschooler knows that! One of the most common questions for homeschool moms is, What will you do for socialization?

School is a perfect environment for children to build community. It's important to note that most developing countries don't have free public school systems. You may want to ask around to find out what schooling options are available. Most schools overseas are classified as private schools, and you will need to pay tuition. Some organizations will provide that funding if there is a school available. Some countries don't have schools at all; there may be a missionary teacher, or the families may opt for homeschooling. Lesotho has an American school and other private schools available, but our family opted for homeschooling, which remains the best option for us. As with everything, it is different for each family.

If you decide to go the homeschooling route, be sure you can get your supplies shipped to you somehow unless your books are available in PDF form. With the curriculum we use now, a majority of our books are available for download. We started with *Sonlight*, and I know quite a few missionaries who use that as well, but they are very book heavy—and those books are heavy! It is necessary to consider shipping costs when selecting your curriculum.

Many missionary wives also develop relationships through their children's school, be it private school or homeschool. Much like in America, relationships with other parents with kids in the same school seem to develop naturally. There is an instant commonality and regular contact during drop-off and pickup. Even if you opt for homeschooling, it is natural to connect with other homeschooling moms and perhaps even develop a co-op. No matter which avenue you decide is best for your family, remember that it is okay to reevaluate throughout the year to determine whether you are still on the right path for you and your kids.

Jesus with Skin On

No matter how your community develops, the most critical aspect is love—love for others, and love for yourself. Jesus told us to love our neighbor as ourselves (Matthew 22:39). But He also gave a new command to "love one another: just as I have loved you, you also are to love one another" (John 13:34). He was telling His disciples to go and be Jesus with skin on.

I've discussed others being there for me, but I wanted to love back too. At times I used my gifts and talents in massage to love others by helping them with pain relief. That was nice for them and me, but I realized there were more ways to love others than just practical. One way I feel loved is when someone spends time with me and encourages me. I wanted to love others the way they felt loved, so I would take time to learn about them. I had one friend who felt loved when people helped her with household chores. Sitting with her and chatting while folding her laundry was helping us both feel loved.

I pray you will develop those deep relationships and forge those lasting bonds so that you can be Jesus with skin on for someone else, and they can be Jesus with skin on for you too. Being missional is about sharing Christ with all people in your community. A Scripture passage that has helped me keep a Christ-focused perspective is this:

> Above all, keep loving one another earnestly, since love covers a multitude of sins. Show hospitality to one another without grumbling. As each has received a gift, use it to serve one another, as good stewards of God's varied grace: whoever speaks, as one who speaks oracles of God; whoever serves, as one who serves by the strength that God supplies—in order that in everything God may be glorified through

Jesus Christ. To him belong glory and dominion forever and ever. Amen. (1 Peter 4:8–11)

Through all the adjustments you will have to make in your journey with adapting to a new culture, setting up a home, and beginning your missionary work, it's important to remind yourself of what matters most—a community of Christ. I spoke in an earlier chapter about the military feeling like a revolving door of friendship. Missions can also feel that way as we each arrive overseas at different times and in different seasons of life. But just because a friend leaves the field doesn't mean the relationship has to end. On the contrary, friendships forged overseas form a solid bond that distance will not easily break. Even if months pass by between talking, that relationship—your community—can stand firm if you want it to.

Reflection:
Think about your current community situation.
- What are some instances when you have had to rely on your community?
- What is your desire for community overseas?
- What are some things you can do to be proactive even at building community before you move?

If you have kids, or are planning to have kids, consider them for a moment.
- What are your plans for school?
- Will you research private schools, or will you homeschool?
- What is your plan for a curriculum?

Think about what it means to be like Jesus.
- What are some ways you can be Jesus with skin on for others? Maybe even for someone today?

I invite you to pray with me.

Prayer:
Father God, I pray you would go before me and prepare the community you have for me. I pray that you would open the hearts of those I will

be doing life with, both on my team and in the extended expat and national community. Please prepare my heart to develop friendships and help me cultivate a spirit that puts relationships before tasks. I also pray you would guide and direct me to the correct path for schooling options for my kids. I pray in Jesus's name, amen.

CHAPTER 10

Spiritual Warfare

*Our victory is not in avoiding tribulation but standing firm in
our faith as we walk through it.*

WOKE UP AND GENTLY RUBBED my growing belly. It had been
about four months since we had returned to Lesotho after our home
assignment, and the baby girl we hoped and prayed for would be
arriving in about a month. I sat on the edge of the bed and whispered
another prayer of thanks before starting my day. My almost-four-year-
old son came in and wrapped his arms as far as he could around my
middle. "Mornin', mama!" Then he patted my tummy and bent down
and gave it a little kiss, "Mornin', sissy!" My heart melted.

When I stood up, the baby dropped low and rested in my pelvis.
Wow, she's getting ready already. As I made my way to the bathroom,
I grabbed a few baby items and added them to one of the boxes in
the corner of the room. It was late September, and Bryan and I were
preparing to go to Johannesburg to await the birth of our daughter.
Since we would be up there for over a month, we had much to bring,
so we packed up over the next two days. I hadn't felt much activity
from her in that time, but I was pretty active myself, so I hadn't paid
much attention.

Tuesday, we began our six-hour drive, and pretty much all I could
do was pay attention. By the time we arrived at our accommodations,

my concern had increased. Once we settled in, I called our midwife. "I haven't felt the baby move in a while."

She suggested we go to the clinic for an examination. "It's probably nothing. We just want to be sure." But I heard the concern in her voice.

After two previous miscarriages, the fear of losing our baby never really went away, but since I had just hit the thirty-six-week gestation mark, we thought we were in the clear, and we could begin to relax. Now I was starting to wonder.

The ultrasound technician came in cheerfully. She squeezed the ice-cold goop onto my skin and began moving her wand across my belly. "Let's take a look at this baby girl!"

My heart crept up in my throat. My eyes darted back and forth from the screen to Bryan, back to the screen, to the technician—her face once joyful, now stoic. Her joy turned to sadness. I squeezed Bryan's hand. Breath was sucked from everyone in the room. The midwife suggested calling the doctor and trying another machine. Any embers of hope that suggestion offered were quickly snuffed out when I heard the four most devastating words an expectant mother could ever hear. "There is no heartbeat."

Our much-prayed-for baby girl, Adia Grace, was gone at thirty-six weeks before ever taking a breath.

A Weapon Not Wielded

We returned to Lesotho after being in Johannesburg for a month. Shortly after our return, some friends came to our house and disclosed some troubling news. My pulse pounded in my ears, almost blocking out their voices as they told stories that had to be out of a Frank Peretti novel. We learned that one of our employees, who had grown up in a village known for witchcraft, had been practicing witchcraft against our family. In addition, she would yell at our son when I was not home. She didn't want us to have more children, so she would lay down lines of muti (a term used for the herbs they used for witchcraft) with the idea that when I stepped over them, I would miscarry.

I stood and began to pace as memories of tragedy and loss filled my mind. This person was someone we had welcomed into our family, given a key to our home, and trusted to watch over our son when I needed to run errands. Heat rose through my neck and into my face as my blood boiled within me. My ears felt as if they were engulfed in flames. *Did this have anything to do with the things that have happened to us here? What right does she have to try to control whether we have more children or not? Who is she to do this to us? We have been so kind and generous to her for years. What would possess her to do such a thing? Oh yeah . . . Satan.*

Even though the concept of spiritual warfare was not foreign to us, this revelation caught us off guard. We knew witchcraft was prevalent in Lesotho, and we knew that some of the people worshiped Satan. We had even prepared for spiritual battle before coming. We had friends pray with us and for us. They prepared us and taught us how to pray against spiritual attacks. But we allowed ourselves to get comfortable, letting down our defenses as if spiritual warfare would not—or could not—touch us.

It was like we had the weapon, cleaned and polished, ready to use, but when we arrived, we hung it neatly above our door. It looked nice and gave the impression we were prepared, but we never took it out of its sheath. Much like having a Bible sitting neatly on the table, it looks nice and gives the impression that we believe in the Word of God, but if we never open it, it is not doing much good. Now we stood face-to-face with the reality that we had an enemy actively trying to drive a wedge between our hearts and God. It was time to engage.

Finding Middle Ground

The terms *spiritual warfare, spiritual attack, spiritual battle,* and the like bring up differing opinions and worldviews and can be a very polarizing subject within the church. The idea of spiritual warfare is foreign to some, ludicrous to others, and many believe the devil is behind everything. Many Bible-believing people don't understand the concept, so they avoid it. Others believe that it doesn't affect us as Christians. In the book *The Essential Guide to Spiritual Warfare*, written by Neil Anderson and Timothy Warner, Mr. Warner writes:

> *Satan creates evil by* perverting what God created to be good, and he does this by *pushing the truth to extremes in either of two opposite directions.* This can be demonstrated on almost any subject one cares to explore, but on the subject of demons *it comes down to the idea that demons are either behind everything or behind nothing* . . . But if the truth is somewhere between those extremes, *we need discernment to know what is demonic and what is the result of living in a fallen world.* Such discernment involves a great deal more knowledge and carries much more responsibility than do the easy answers at the extremes.[4]
>
> The Bible itself gives us the balance we need. *Christ is the focus of Scripture.* There are no long passages on demonology. Therefore our primary focus should be on knowing God and His ways. *If we know the truth, then we can easily detect the deceptions of the father of lies.* God didn't reveal Satan's ways or assignments in detail, because they change. Christ is the way, but Satan has many ways. Jesus is the truth; Satan is the father of lies.[5]

Polarization of our society happens with so many subjects, dividing the church with one side saying that you are wrong if you don't believe this way. How many social media posts have you seen with the phrase "If you don't agree with this, unfriend me now"? But things just aren't that black and white. While we need to be alert to the enemy's schemes, we shouldn't focus on them so much that we live in fear or continually look for enemy activity. As Mr. Warner said, if our focus is on knowing God and His ways, we can easily detect the enemy's schemes.

When people talk about spiritual warfare, many envision a gruesome battle with swords drawn and bloodshed. However, when Paul wrote about the armor of God in Ephesians 6, most of the pieces he listed were defensive, used for protection. We need to protect ourselves from the lies of the enemy, which are what cause us to fight each other rather than the real enemy. We are to be in the Word of God daily, continually building our relationship with Him and getting to know who He is—getting to know His truth—and building a solid foundation of faith.

There are only two offensive weapons listed in the armor of God in Ephesians. One is the sword of the Spirit. The second, which is listed right along with it, is prayer. The Scripture says, "Take the helmet of salvation, and the sword of the Spirit, which is the word of God, *praying at all times* in the Spirit, with all prayer and supplication" (Ephesians 6:17–18). We should never underestimate the power of prayer.

Transformation through Tragedy

Once the shock of our discovery waned, we donned our battle armor. We took that sword off the wall, unsheathed it, and took it up in prayer. We prayed through every room in our home, anointing them with oil. We prayed around the perimeter of our property, and we prayed over our son.

When we began praying for our son, something in him flipped. We went from prayer stance to battle stance. He literally kicked and screamed that he didn't want us to pray for him. Some of that could be chalked up to an active four-year-old boy not wanting us to hold him, but this was different. We had never seen him this way before, and it scared us. So we prayed even harder. He continued his physical bouts until about thirty seconds after we said, "In Jesus's name, amen." He didn't squirm to get away as if that was the goal of his kicking and screaming. Instead, he completely relaxed into Bryan's arms. Then we both hugged and kissed him, and when he got down, he went on his merry way as if nothing had happened.

Our friends, Tim and Mindy, who had prepared us and prayed for us before going overseas, had studied spiritual warfare in college, so I called them for prayer and advice. After I shared most of the story, Tim saw a vision. He hesitated to share because it wasn't making sense to him, but Mindy encouraged him to share it anyway. He saw a room-like space with several other rooms connected to it. He wasn't sure what that meant, but there it was. Tim and Mindy had never been to our house in Lesotho, so they couldn't have known that in the middle of our house was a small area—you couldn't even call it a room or a hallway—that connected six rooms of the house. Three bedrooms, a bathroom, the living room, and the kitchen. When I told him about it, Tim encouraged me to pray through that space.

I considered this confirmation that something of the dark spiritual realm was going on in our home. When Bryan and I began to share with our community what was happening and asked for prayer, we had some people who scoffed at us, saying things like, "You think witchcraft is more powerful than Jesus." No, that is not what I think. Did witchcraft cause the death of our daughter? Maybe. We may never know. We still don't know why she died. What I do know is that we were under spiritual attack and that someone we once trusted was performing witchcraft against us. What I don't know is whether or not those are related.

Some may ask, *So, what about my kids always bickering? Is that a spiritual attack?* Well, maybe! If you think about it, we must put on the helmet of salvation to protect us from the enemy's lies. If the enemy's lies can cause strife among grown men and women, there's little room for argument that he could put that same wedge between our little humans. Spiritual attacks come in many forms, and not all attacks are as dramatic as ours. I know some people who have had seemingly more minor struggles, but they hit them in their weak areas, so they were significant. I know some who have gone through much more challenging fights. Not all struggles are spiritual attacks, but praying through them and ensuring you are placing the protection of God around you and your family should always be your first line of defense.

I am not saying the devil is behind everything, nor am I on the other end of the spectrum saying he's not behind anything. This polarization of beliefs is just where the enemy wants us. When Christians are divided on any topic, we lack the unity required to be fruitful for the kingdom of God. When our friend scoffed at me and attacked my beliefs, she caused a rift between us, and the enemy can and will use that to his advantage. For the record, I know that God is more powerful than witchcraft. For whatever reason, the Lord has allowed these things to touch our lives, and now we get to walk through it. I intend to walk through it in prayer.

Holy Spirit Prompted Prayer

Having an employee trying to harm us certainly affected how we viewed the culture, and it took a couple of years before we trusted anyone to come work in our home again. But having friends in the culture, we realized her behavior was not a reflection of the culture as a whole, and neither Bryan nor I hold anger or resentment toward her. We believe she was just a vessel the enemy used to get to our family. Had we held on to bitterness and resentment, that would have given the enemy even more of a foothold to wreak havoc in our life. No matter the enemy's goal, we grew stronger in our faith, closer to one another, and closer to God. We are more aware of the darkness that surrounds us, and now we know to stay alert. That shift in awareness has changed how we view the spiritual world and has made us more sensitive to the Holy Spirit.

An example of this sensitivity came during one of Bryan's typical workdays. Bryan flies small airplanes to isolated villages among rural mountains. The runways are short dirt airstrips cut into those mountains. If he is not focused, it is easy for things to go wrong. One concern for the pilots is runway incursions, which is when someone or something—like an animal—is on the runway and the pilot cannot land, or if he attempted to land, it could cause an accident. These incursions are unpredictable but don't happen often.

Bryan is a very competent pilot, so I don't usually fret, but I felt uneasy about him going to work one day. I wasn't worried, per se; I just felt like it would be a difficult day for him. So I prayed for him and dove into my work. In the middle of a project, something prompted me to pray again. So again I prayed and went about my day. I was led to pray a third time, and that was when I started to get a little concerned, so I sent a text message to Bryan asking him to use an extra measure of caution. I prayed again, but this time instead of resuming my work, I continued praying. When Bryan is flying, he can't respond to messages right away, so I just sent the text and kept praying throughout the day. Though I didn't know what I ought to pray, the Holy Spirit knew, and I just needed to obey.

When Bryan came home that evening, we talked about my prompts to pray, and he shared with me that my prayers were quite timely and necessary. The wind had already made the flying quite challenging, but on top of that, he had encountered three runway incursions that day. As I mentioned, runway incursions are a concern, but they're not frequent. And he'd just had three in one day—on three separate airstrips! Each one happened around the times the Holy Spirit led me to pray.

Would Bryan have been okay if I hadn't prayed? Perhaps. Will I continue to pray for him? You bet! While I know it is crucial to pray for him for his sake, praying also helps me be more connected to the Holy Spirit. The more we communicate with God, the closer we are to Him. The closer we are to Him, the more our hearts, thoughts, and wills are aligned with His. Prayer is powerful, so keep on praying!

Victory in Jesus

Bryan and I were stretched thin our first few years in Lesotho—physically, emotionally, and spiritually. That in itself was enough to feel like we were under attack. Discovering that we were actually under spiritual attack should not have come as a surprise, but we won the victory. "For everyone who has been born of God overcomes the world. And this is the victory that has overcome the world—*our faith*" (1 John 5:4). The victory is not in avoiding tribulation but standing firm in our faith as we walk through it.

When we read the Gospels, Jesus tells us He has overcome the world. Many people focus on the "overcome the world" part of that Scripture and believe Christians should not have trouble. But if we look more closely at what it says just before that, we see that we will have to walk through trials. Jesus says, "I have said these things to you, that in me you may have peace. In the world *you will have tribulation. But take heart; I have overcome the world*" (John 16:33). What Jesus is saying is that trials and tribulation will come, but we have hope and peace in Him to walk through them.

In the gospel of Luke, we read about Jesus sending out seventy-two people to go to the places He was about to go.

> The seventy-two returned with joy, saying, "Lord, even the demons are subject to us in your name!" And he said to them, "I saw Satan fall like lightning from heaven. Behold, *I have given you authority* to tread on serpents and scorpions, and over all the power of the enemy, and nothing shall hurt you. Nevertheless, *do not rejoice in this, that the spirits are subject to you,* but *rejoice that your names are written in heaven.*" (Luke 10:17–20)

So, we don't rejoice in that Jesus has given us authority, but we rejoice in that our names are written in heaven. We dare not seek out spiritual warfare, but we need not fear it either.

Maybe you are unsure how to engage in spiritual warfare, you may not understand it, or perhaps you've never even heard about it until now. Being unknown or misunderstood, it can often bring fear. When I first became a Christian, I didn't hear much about it. Once I did start hearing about it, I didn't understand it, and I can't say I fully understand it now, but I couldn't ignore it. This battle is not something to fear but something to be prepared for.

I am not a scholar of spiritual warfare. I can only speak from my experience and what I've read. If you would like to learn more about it, I suggest reading one of the many books about understanding spiritual warfare and how to protect yourself and fight against the enemy. The one I quoted earlier is a great place to start, *The Essential Guide to Spiritual Warfare* by Neil Anderson and Timothy Warner. Spiritual warfare is not something we seek out, but something that is going on all around us all the time, no matter where in the world we are.

Armor Up

Whether we see it or not, whether we believe it or not, there *is* a battle going on in the heavenly places. "For we do not wrestle against flesh and blood, but against the rulers, against the authorities, against the cosmic powers over this present darkness, against the spiritual forces of evil in the heavenly places" (Ephesians 6:12). Sadly, some cultures do worship Satan and perform witchcraft. Their attacks may not have power over us because Jesus has given us authority over the enemy (Luke 10:19), but we still have the responsibility to execute that authority as followers of Christ. We don't need to fear the spiritual battle, but it is irresponsible to behave as if it is not happening.

As we pray for discernment to be *aware* of the schemes of the devil, let us all put on the whole armor of God that we may be able to *stand against* the schemes of the devil as well (Ephesians 6:11, paraphrased). Putting on the armor of God should be a daily task. When you wake up in the morning, you know you have to get dressed. You don't say it; it's just a daily task. You also understand why you get dressed. It is socially preferred. Can you picture yourself putting on the armor of God as a daily routine? At first, you may need to remind yourself why you are putting on the armor of God, but you can think of it as getting dressed spiritually. You can mentally practice it just in the process of getting dressed in the morning.

Let's put the passage of Ephesians 6 in the order of a daily routine:
- Before you get dressed, you have to *stand*. "Therefore take up the whole armor of God, that you may be able to withstand in the evil day, and having done all, to *stand firm*" (v.13).
- As you put on your *pants*, picture the *belt of truth*. "Stand therefore, having fastened on the *belt of truth*" (v.14).
- As you put on your *shirt,* picture the *breastplate of righteousness*. "And having put on the *breastplate of righteousness*" (v. 14).
- As you put on your *shoes*, picture the *gospel of peace*. "And, as *shoes* for your feet, having put on the *readiness* given by the *gospel of peace*" (v.15).

- As you put on your *jacket,* it will *shield* you from the weather. "In all circumstances take up the *shield of faith,* with which you can extinguish all the flaming darts of the evil one" (v.16).
- As you *brush your hair,* you can picture putting on the *helmet of salvation.* "Take the *helmet of salvation*" (v.17).
- As you take up your *phone,* picture taking up a *sword.* "Take . . . the *sword of the Spirit,* which is the *word of God*" (v.17).
- As you do your *mental checklist,* say a *prayer.* "*Praying* at all times in the Spirit, with all prayer and supplication" (v.18).
- As you grab your morning *coffee,* it will wake you up and keep you *alert.* "*Keep alert* with all perseverance, making supplication for all the saints" (v.18).

And just like that, you are ready for the day!

Many forget those last two powerful pieces of the armor of God, staying alert and praying. Those who deny spiritual warfare are typically those who are not alert. They are asleep to what is going on around them. Satan has no problem with people denying he's at work because that just makes his job easier. Staying alert is one of the best ways to protect yourself.

Prayer can help us stay alert. We can pray for God to open our eyes to the spiritual world around us and for Him to teach us how to engage in the battle through prayer. God calls us to be in continual prayer. Bryan and I continue to pray over our home, praying specifically to break curses that the enemy may have cast. Every night we pray the Lord would not let anything that is not of Him disturb our family or our home. We pray continually throughout the day just to be connected to God, not solely in response to the enemy. The more we practice, the more it becomes second nature, and the less we have to think about it; we just do it. Let's be diligent in doing our part in the battle for the kingdom of God.

Reflection:
Think about what Scripture says about the battle in the spiritual realm.

- What do you know or believe about spiritual warfare?
- What are some things you can do now to learn more about spiritual battles?

Think about some hardships you've faced.

- What are some areas where you have felt you have been under spiritual attack?
- In what ways have you grown from the trials you have faced?

Think about the mental practice of putting on the armor of God.

- What can you put into practice today to put on the full armor of God every day?
- What can you do to remind yourself to put on the armor each day?
- What pieces of the armor do you tend to neglect?

Think about what goes on around you every day.

- What do you need to change to stay alert to spiritual warfare?
- How can you incorporate those into your daily life?
- What are some ways you can remind yourself to be praying throughout the day?

I invite you to pray with me.

Prayer:

Father God, I confess I have been asleep, and I pray that you would open my eyes to the spiritual battle going on around me. I know that not everything is an attack from the enemy. I pray you would help me discern if something happened because of my poor choices or if it is a spiritual attack. I pray you would teach me how to put on the full armor of God and be protected and prepared to fight. Please help me to stay alert and be in prayer continually. I pray in Jesus's name, amen.

CHAPTER II

Life after Death

If we stay in the pain of what might have been or pine for what might be, we lose the ability to enjoy the gift of what is.

I TOOK MY PHONE OUT OF my pocket, and my hands began to tremble when I saw the caller ID. We had been anticipating this call for eight months. Despite my disdain for talking on the phone, I pressed the accept button, and my voice cracked a hopeful "Hello?" My friend, the new director at the orphanage, responded, her voice filled with joyful tears, "I'm not supposed to tell you this, but I wanted to be the one to share the news—you've been matched!" The phone almost slipped from my grip as her words sank in. Less than a year after Adia's death, God was gifting us with another daughter.

Not quite two years earlier, I couldn't have imagined this was where we would be. After two miscarriages and getting no answers from the fertility specialist, Bryan and I were not sure I would be able to get pregnant again or that I would be able to carry a child to term if we did conceive.

A few months after our second miscarriage, we sat on my brother's couch reading a book one of our friends had given us. We had barely finished the first chapter when I turned to Bryan and said, "We're supposed to adopt, aren't we?"

"I think so," he responded quizzically. We had discussed the idea for years but determined adoption was what other people did, not us.

We talked and prayed over the next few weeks and finally decided to start the adoption process when we returned to Lesotho. We were excited about the prospect of growing our family through adoption. We began researching books and articles. We reached out to our friends who had adopted before us. We asked them endless questions, trying to understand what this decision would mean for our family. In just a few short weeks, the once surreal prospect of adoption started to become real.

Just about three weeks after that January day when God called us to adopt, tears filled my eyes as I showed Bryan the home pregnancy tests—I had taken two because I couldn't believe it. Air was sucked from our lungs as we stared at the word "Pregnant." I couldn't tell which was more powerful, the excitement of having another baby or the fear of losing another one—or the question mark this put on our adoption plans . . . though not a question of if, but of when. We decided that after we delivered the baby, we would still go ahead with adoption. Though Adia's arrival took a different turn than expected, we held to our decision after taking a few months to process and grieve.

Grief and Forgiveness

Adia's passing brought questions to many facets of our life. We questioned whether or not we should try to conceive again and if we were making the right choice to follow through on our decision to adopt. We even wondered if we should stay in Lesotho. Friends also questioned our determination to move forward with adoption since we submitted our application just a few months after Adia's death. However, we had made our decision to adopt before Adia died. Yes, we were still grieving—that is a never-ending process—but life doesn't stop because we are in pain.

People are encouraged to give themselves time to grieve during a time of loss, but grief is a lot like forgiveness. They are both different for everyone. Most of us understand that we should forgive others for the wrongs they have done to us and forgive ourselves for the mistakes we have made, but what do we do when there is no one to accuse? As we grieve, we forgive what happened, even though we don't know where to place the blame. Only then can we move forward. Grief and forgiveness are the same in that you have to walk through both one day at a time.

The knowledge that someone had been performing witchcraft against us did cause us to question why in the world we were in a country where the people want to inflict pain on us. The simple response was because that was where God called us to be. We stayed in obedience because God didn't call us to leave. There is no guarantee returning to America would magically make life better or easier or that we would have avoided these trials had we been living in America. Whether or not witchcraft caused Adia's death or our two earlier miscarriages does not matter when we look at the big picture. Choosing to walk in forgiveness gives us the freedom and power to continue in the ministry God called us to.

Maybe you are caught up in the grief of something that has happened in your life. Perhaps you are even holding resentment toward someone who has wronged you. I am not telling you to get over it; that's just insensitive. No, I know you can't just get over it. Humans don't work that way. But just as choosing to forgive someone for a wrong done to us frees us from the bondage of bitterness, so too in the process of grieving, forgiving an event or situation that brought us pain frees us to enjoy the present moment we call life.

Many times we cannot control the things that happen in our lives, but we can choose how we respond to them. Peter tells us,

> Beloved, do not be surprised at the fiery trial when it comes upon you to test you, as though something strange were happening to you. But rejoice insofar as you share Christ's sufferings, that you may also rejoice and be glad when his glory is revealed. (1 Peter 4:12–13)

Rejoice and be glad when his glory is revealed. Again, this is not a get-over-it kind of thing. But we can trust that in His time, God will reveal His glory through the trial, and we will rejoice and be glad.

Learning to Trust

The loss of our child was unlike any pain we had experienced before. The sorrow was deep and paralyzing at times, yet walking through this valley strengthened our faith in God, our relationship with Him, our relationship with each other, and brought a beautiful season of growth. A friend of ours says, "You cannot appreciate joy without sorrow, nor sorrow without joy." Through our sorrow, we saw God's hand working in so many ways to bring us joy. We started seeing all the ways God carried us through the good in our lives, not just tragedy. In that, we find new hope and new comfort each day.

When Adia passed away, a friend drove the six hours to Johannesburg to be with us. As we waited for the doctor, she said to us, "I can't tell you why this has happened, but I will say, God trusts you with this pain." At the time, those words didn't make much sense. Of course, what does make sense when you are overwhelmed with sorrow? As we walked through our mourning, we would often reflect on those words, "God trusts you with this pain," and God began to bring clarity. God trusts us to press into Him and allow His glory to shine through our sorrow. He trusts us to keep our hope in Him, to rest our weary souls on His shoulder, and to let Him comfort us. He trusts us to show others that, although there is sorrow, our joy comes from the Lord.

I am already slow to learn some of the lessons God has for me. Learning to trust Him when absolutely nothing in my life seems to make sense has been one of the more challenging and continual lessons I have faced. God brought us through our struggles in some unexpected ways, like friends driving six hours to support us, people giving us a pertinent Scripture verse at just the right moment, teammates bringing us meals or other items to cheer us up, cards from our friends in America, and calls from those who just wanted to check in. All of these reminded us just how important our community is.

To trust God fully, I have to be in tune with Him. Jesus says, "The Holy Spirit, whom the Father will send in my name, he will teach you all things and bring to your remembrance all that I have said to you" (John 14:26). The Holy Spirit comforts us and reminds us of the goodness and promises of God. I must continually be in the Word of God to remind me of His character and His promises. I must forgive the pain of the trials, walk in faith through the healing, and let go of my need for answers.

Living without Answers

I am confident I am not alone in wanting to know the why behind the bad things that happen, but simply put, we live in a fallen world, and sometimes there is no why. I had friends ask how God could let this happen to us, "of all people," when we are "over there serving Him." That simple question sparked doubt in my mind about God. I questioned why He let this happen to us, why other people were having babies just fine, and why we had lost three. Why have we experienced so much loss and hardship when we were walking in obedience to God's call?

I don't think those questions are wrong, but when they cause us to doubt the goodness of God, that gives the enemy a foothold into our hearts and allows even more room for doubt. And that's what the enemy likes to do, put just enough doubt in our minds about the goodness of God. That's why being in the Word of God is so important! We need to resist the devil and his lies and schemes and remember God's promises.

James talks about both of these: "Submit yourselves therefore to God. Resist the devil, and he will flee from you" (James 4:7) and "Blessed is the man who remains steadfast under trial, for when he has stood the test he will receive the crown of life, which God has promised to those who love him" (James 1:12). Being a missionary or Christian in any capacity does not exempt us from the trials of life—God's Word says just the opposite. Nevertheless, we can resist the devil, persevere in sufferings, and receive the crown of life promised to us!

There's a saying that God doesn't give us more than we can handle. I don't believe that. If we could manage everything on our own, we wouldn't need to depend on God. I wonder if that phrase came from a misunderstanding of 1 Corinthians 10:14, where it says, "No temptation has overtaken you that is not common to man. God is faithful, and *he will not let you be tempted beyond your ability*, but with the temptation he will also provide the way of escape, that you may be able to endure it." This passage says He will not allow us to be *tempted* beyond our ability—not that our trials would not be beyond our ability. Even still, it is God who provides a way of escape! When the enemy tempts me to believe the lies, God provides a way out through His Word.

- When I begin to doubt God's goodness, His Word reminds me, "The Lord is gracious and merciful, slow to anger and abounding in steadfast love. The Lord is good to all, and his mercy is over all that he has made" (Psalm 145:8–9).
- When tempted to believe He caused this pain as punishment, Scripture says, "All we like sheep have gone astray; we have turned—every one—to his own way and the Lord has laid on [Jesus] the iniquity of us all" (Isaiah 53:6), reminding us that any punishment due to us by God, Jesus willingly took on that penalty for us.
- When tempted to believe He could never use this pain for anything good, His Word says, "And we know that in all things God works for the good of those who love him, who have been called according to his purpose" (Romans 8:28).

We may never have answers to the many questions we have. I wonder what would change if I did? Would it change how I look at things to know why Adia died? If we went back to before she was born or conceived and God said, "Your daughter is going to die because . . ." would we go along and say, "Okay, God, let's do this"? I don't think anyone would willingly sign up for suffering even if they knew why it was happening. Though I suppose, as Christians, that is what we do, right? But it's usually better if we don't know what's coming.

I wonder if things have happened in your life that have left more questions than answers. If we continually demand answers to those questions, we close ourselves off from the good that can come from our trials, and we give the enemy a foothold into our hearts, becoming less effective for the kingdom of God. His Word reminds me that even though He allowed this hardship to touch our lives, it is out of love and for a greater purpose, not out of an evil joy of seeing us suffer.

Glimpses of Redemption

Many heroes of the Bible suffered greatly, and God used their pain for His glory. Lazarus died! Mary and Martha sent word to Jesus saying, "'Lord, he whom you love is ill.' But when Jesus heard it, he said, 'This illness does not lead to death. *It is for the glory of God*, so that the Son of God may be glorified through it'" (John 11:3–4). After Lazarus died, Jesus wept. He weeps with us when we suffer as well.

Just before Jesus raised Lazarus from the tomb, he said to Martha,

> "Did I not tell you that if you believed you would see the glory of God?" So they took away the stone. And Jesus lifted up his eyes and said, "Father, I thank you that you have heard me. I knew that you always hear me, but *I said this on account of the people standing around, that they may believe that you sent me*." (John 11:40–42)

God used the death and resurrection of Lazarus for His glory, a little foreshadowing to how He would use the death and resurrection of His Son for His glory.

Joseph also endured his share of suffering. When he was sold into slavery, his brothers allowed their father to believe he was dead, but God used Joseph's experience to save the lives of many people in Egypt, including the brothers who betrayed him. "As for you, you meant evil against me, but God meant it for good, to bring it about that many people should be kept alive, as they are today" (Genesis 50:20). No matter what we suffer, we all hope to see God redeem the pain we have endured. We hope to see some good come from losses that leave a chasm in our hearts. I think redemption is all around us, but we might have to look for it.

As we processed and walked through our grief, God gave us little glimpses of how He has redeemed some of our pain. Bryan's dad and stepmom came out to South Africa to support us when Adia died. Shortly after they left, Dad had a dream he didn't share with us until about two months before we got matched for adoption. Adia came to him in his dream and told him she had picked out a sister to be part of our family. Then he saw a vision of his granddaughter-to-be, who would have brown skin, a round head, and big, brown, round eyes. When we met the daughter they matched us with, it was almost as if they had painted a picture of Dad's dream. Having our adopted daughter match the vision in Dad's dream was a little glimpse that this was part of God's plan.

That may not seem like much in the grand scheme of things, but there's more. Early in our marriage, Bryan and I desperately prayed for children. We thought it would happen right away, but it took a while. In my prayers one night, God reminded me that children were a gift from Him. So we decided that whenever God decided to give us children, we would find names that mean "gift." We found the name Adia first, which means "gift" in Swahili. When we found out we were having a boy for my first pregnancy, we found the name Matthias, which means "gifted by God." When we had been in Lesotho for about a year, he was given the Sesotho name Mpho (Mm Po), which also means "gift." The name they gave our adopted daughter at the orphanage was the Sesotho name Dimpho (Dim Po), which is the plural of Mpho, meaning "gifts." We named her Isabella Faith Dimpho—we call her Bella. She pluralized the gifts of children in our family.

One could explain that away because that is a fairly common name in Lesotho. By itself, sure, we could call it a coincidence. But let me add in this last bit of information that sticks with me and adds to the hope that God will continue to redeem our story. When children arrive at the orphanage, they don't typically come with birth certificates or notes about their lives. It's an educated guessing game to determine how old they are or what their medical history is. Based on their growth, the medical staff estimates their age and chooses a birth date in that range. The birth date they picked for Bella is the same date as Adia's death the same year. The bittersweetness of that day does not escape me. But on that day, rather than living in grief and mourning Adia's death, we get to celebrate Bella's birth.

I could go on and on about the little things. These little glimpses of redemption give me hope that Adia's death was not in vain. They assure me that God does have great plans for us, and we can be joyful for the time she was in the womb. What a beautiful picture of joy kissing sorrow and a wonderful reminder that we can't fully appreciate joy without experiencing sorrow.

Room for a New Dream

For some time after we adopted Bella, I still longed for more children. Every month, I would ride the emotional roller coaster of hope and disappointment as my prayer was continually left unanswered. I was pining for the desires of my heart, hoping beyond hope God would answer my prayers the way I wanted Him to until I noticed that my sadness and disappointment kept me from enjoying the gifts God had already given me. So I stopped.

Instead of praying for Him to fulfill the desires of my heart, I prayed for Him to help me line up my desires with His. Instead of praying for more children, I prayed He would help me enjoy the two children we had. Instead of praying for Him to heal my body, I prayed He would help me enjoy doing the things I could do. Instead of asking Him to fulfill the dream I longed for, I prayed for Him to give me a new one. I have realized that letting go of an unfulfilled dream isn't giving up hope. It is simply making room in my heart for a new dream.

If I continue to grieve what I've lost or continue yearning for what I want, I get stuck. My new hope is to stay in the present and enjoy the gifts I have. My prayer is that I would forgive the hurt of the past and remember Adia for the door she opened to allow more joy in our lives. If we remain in the pain of what might have been or pine for what might be, we lose the ability to enjoy the gift of what is.

Elisabeth Elliot said, "We want to avoid suffering, death, sin, ashes. But we live in a world crushed and broken and torn, a world God Himself visited to redeem. We receive His poured-out life, and being allowed the high privilege of suffering with Him may then pour ourselves out for others." My new prayer is that I may honor God in pouring myself out for others and to "be joyful in hope, patient in affliction, faithful in prayer" (Romans 12:12).

The dream I had in my heart for more children was not in the cards for us, but God has given me a new dream: to be a wife who is present for my husband, a mom who is present for my children, and a friend to walk alongside others. My new dream may seem simple, but sometimes simple is better. It frees up my emotions to walk through this fallen world alongside others and pray through their hurts, sit with them when there are no words, and hopefully be a light to help them see the glimpses of redemption in their own lives. I pray God may reveal His glory to others through my life.

God's Glory Revealed

We can find our comfort and strength in the Lord. Scripture says God sent Jesus "to heal the brokenhearted, to comfort all who mourn, to give them beauty for ashes, the oil of joy for mourning, that they may be called trees of righteousness, the planting of the Lord, that He may be glorified" (Isaiah 61:1–3). *That they may be called trees of righteousness.* Trees are strong, but they don't start that way. They develop their strength through harsh winds and mighty storms.

Sometimes I watch how the trees bend during a storm and wonder how they stay rooted! Perhaps that is what God wants for us, that when others witness how we walk through our trials and suffering, they will see how we hold up, that they will discover how we remain rooted in Him and see that the Lord is our strength and hope, and that would bring hope to them as well. I don't claim that we walked through our grief perfectly—if there is such a thing. Grief is messy. But we grew stronger as our roots spread deeper into the soil of God's word. I pray that we honored God through it, and I pray our lives continue to glorify Him.

As you reflect on the storms and trials you have walked through, take a moment to focus on areas where you have grown stronger. Think about the areas where you feel stuck and how you might be able to shift your focus to walk in forgiveness of that pain. If you are currently walking through a storm of pain, God sees you. Lean into the One who will keep you grounded. Stay rooted in Christ. Press into Him and know that He trusts you with this pain, and He will use it for His glory and for your good.

Reflection:
Think about hardships or betrayals you've been through.
- In what areas might you be withholding forgiveness?
- In what areas of your life do you feel the effects of bitterness?

Think about your circumstances that make you question your faith.
- What do you need to do so you can fully trust God?
- In what areas could seeing a counselor help you move forward?

Think about questions you have that have gone unanswered.
- What answers are you longing for that you have to learn to live without?
- How do you see God's glory shining through those struggles?
- In what ways have your struggles strengthened your faith?

I invite you to pray with me.

Prayer:
Father God, I want to lay my pain at your feet and surrender it to you. I don't want to be stuck in my grief anymore. Lord, I don't know why I've had to endure this pain. Even if I did, I don't think I would sign on for it. Lord, show me how this will make me stronger and help me let go of my need for answers. Help me to trust you to redeem my suffering. Help me to glorify your name as I walk through these trials, to allow you to be my comfort and my strength, to walk in the freedom that forgiveness brings. I pray In Jesus's name, amen.

CHAPTER 12

Dancing with the Father

*We can see the beauty in the sorrow for the joy that comes after it
and redemption in the little things that reveal God's glory.*

A YOUNG WOMAN WITH HER ARMS stretched wide spins through a boundless green meadow flecked with wildflowers. Her tanned skin makes a stark contrast under the white spaghetti straps of her A-line summer dress. The bottom of her dress dances with the wind, flaring out to look like the tutu of a ballerina. A soft smile rests on her face as she twirls through the spindly stems. She closes her eyes and breathes in the mixed scents of flowers and fresh grass. She turns once more and bounds through the meadow like a doe through a forest, freely dancing with the Father to music only He and she can hear. She comes to a stop under the shade of a large oak tree, and her silhouette disappears as she collapses in sweet surrender to the tall grass that swallows her.

I believe that woman is you! The journey of following God brings sweet freedom like spinning through a meadow of wildflowers dancing to music you and God have created together. You sway to and fro. The melody is ebbing and flowing, rising and falling, surging through a dramatic crescendo to a stark pause—a dreamlike peace beyond understanding. You may get out of step, you may even fall, but God will gently pull you up, brush the dirt off your beautiful dress, and tend to the scrape on your knee. He will situate your feet back on top of His, and you will pick up where you left off. The tumble may leave a scar or two, but He tends to those as well, making them beautiful reminders of His grace and mercy.

Let's think of the parts of the missionary journey as a symphony. When you listen to the music of a symphony, you can hear all the different segments dancing together. Some parts will move faster, some will move slower, some will be louder, and some will be softer. Sometimes things will seem like excessive noise, and other times, the silence will be deafening. Some aspects may not be easy while you're in the midst of them, but when you look back, you will see just how essential each piece is and how all the segments dance together. Through it all, if you stay in tune with the Father, you will appreciate the beautiful orchestration you and God created together.

As we review our first few segments of this book, we can think of them as our foundation, learning the basics. The elements of the rest of the chapters will come dancing along. Musicians don't just go out on stage and perform a beautiful symphony without putting in some work. They read the sheet music, learn the notes, memorize the tune, and practice. They get a feel for the tempo and find a rhythm with the other elements of the overall composition. So we begin with the flexibility to be learners, adapting and adjusting to God's plan. God is the conductor. If we make a mistake, God will correct us and guide us in the right direction.

We take in all the new information as if reading sheet music. It may seem like a jumbled mess of dots when it's coming at us so fast, but once we get it organized, it starts to make sense. Scripture tells us to address one another "in psalms and hymns and spiritual songs, singing and making melody to the Lord with your heart" (Ephesians 5:19). As we share our ministry ideas with family, friends, and churches and ask for support, we invite other people's music into our symphony.

A Time to Dance

We want the music to dance and carry us along. We can't move if we keep our feet planted on the floor—or in the world, our job, or our home. But if we root ourselves in Christ, we can go where He calls us to go. We can be confident of our steps—our call to missions—but still follow Christ's lead. That means holding our plans loosely, submitting to Him, and allowing His music to move us in the right direction. We can be flexible, not set in our ways. As we stay in tune with God's ways, we can hear from the Holy Spirit and follow His direction.

> For everything there is a season, and a time for every matter under heaven: a time to be born, and a time to die; *a time to plant, and a time to pluck up what is planted*; a time to kill, and a time to heal; a time to break down, and a time to build up; a time to weep, and a time to laugh; a time to mourn, and *a time to dance*. (Ecclesiastes 1:1–4).

When the music pauses, we can be patient in that season as we wait for God to clarify the mission He has for us and walk in that purpose to His glory. The things we do for God are not to earn His love, but they pour out because of the love He has lavished on us.

God is the best dance partner to have because He knows all our weaknesses, and He will either allow us to sidestep them or help us grow in them. We can embrace the brokenness that brought us to God as it gives us a unique perspective to share His love with others in whatever capacity we find ourselves. Being in step with God keeps us in step with our spouses as we learn to work from home together and clarify our expectations. Our music synchronizes with their music, and our melodies dance together as we forge this adventure together.

As we prepare for moving and saying goodbye, our music grows more somber as we part ways with friends and family. Once we arrive on the field, we hear the melodies of our new community, those on our team, and in our extended expat and national community, more prominently. As we learn their steps and how they do things, we discover where we fit and how we can contribute, learning more about ourselves and our gifts in the process. We never silence the music of our family and friends in our home culture, but it plays on in the background.

Finding the Rhythm

Musicians don't practice just one piece of music. They practice the components that make up the music, like scales. Likewise, we can take care of some components that make up our person by establishing good exercise and eating habits, creating a foundation that will flow naturally into other aspects of life. We can also minimize the stress of an overseas move by preparing for travel—coordinating the trip, packing, and planning for rest and entertainment, thus minimizing the interruption of the rhythm of our music.

With any musical piece, part of the learning is doing. As we jump into our new culture, it will feel awkward at times. We will go through the various stages of culture shock until we find a groove, a rhythm that syncs with ours. We will learn to embrace the changes and understand that nothing will stay the same. We can have guest musicians, like a counselor, on standby, so we have someone to walk through the transition with us. They can give us coping techniques and ways to thrive, which will help us find the rhythm of our new culture.

Our music will ebb and flow throughout our entire journey overseas. We know that we will never fit in because we are not of this world, but we can still learn to move with the music. We will find the things we enjoy as a family, and we will do them often. We can enjoy the fun moments to the fullest and learn to laugh about the frustrations. We invite dance partners as we build our community and find a rhythm with them as well. Our family may have a different melody, but we can still work in harmony.

As we create this beautiful synchronization with God and others, we will be more aware of the off-key notes of lies and deceptions of the enemy. They are so foul-sounding that they won't fit into the music we are orchestrating with God. We can dance in confidence as we put on the whole armor of God each day. Even though it is battle gear, we can still dance with grace. We can hear the prompts of the Holy Spirit, and we can armor up and pray without losing a step.

We may stumble, the enemy may trip us, but we can pick ourselves up and get back in the dance. We can resist the devil, and he will flee.

We can remind ourselves of God's promises and embrace our challenges as we grow in faith and strength. If someone wrongs us, we can forgive. If we are hurt by something that happened, we can grieve and forgive the event. We can learn to live without answers, knowing that they can't undo what's happened. We can see the beauty in the sorrow for the joy that comes after it, the redemption in the little things we see every day that reveal God's glory.

Enjoy the Music

I hope that taking care of these foundations will allow you to focus more on your spiritual life, which surprisingly often is neglected as people prepare to go on the mission field. People can get so wrapped up in support raising, speaking events, and sharing about what they will be doing that they neglect their relationship with the One they are doing it for.

You have a unique composition of music that is just between you and God. Your husband has his own as well. You are in this orchestration together, and his music plays along with yours. While your arrangements are in harmony with one another, they are not the same. Sometimes you will need to rest together, and sometimes you will rest separately and let the other take the lead. But the Lord plays on. He may be silent at times, but resist the urge to fill the silence. It may come across like that misplaced note during a dramatic pause.

It's difficult to close a book when the story continues, but here I sit, trying to wrap it up in a bow like the ending of a Hallmark movie, trying to give you a picture of what God has done in and through our life in just twelve short chapters. It's not the length of the story but the depth. In just eight years, God has brought us through some challenging trials. I don't want to focus on the degree of difficulty but the fact that God carried us through them. He didn't just walk with us. Much like the "Footprints" poem, God carried us when we needed help. And he continues to do so!

I've learned that no matter the trials we go through in our life, God is there. When we hear the crashing cymbals and drums pounding in our ears as we walk through the valley of hardships, we may fear there is no end in sight. But when the drumming stops, the music pauses as we catch our breath. We look up to the mountain from where our help comes and hear the sound of dancing violins as we walk out of the valley into God's glory. God showed me that there is a time to grieve—a pause in the symphony. And there is a time to move forward as the music gently picks back up to a pace fitting for each day. The rhythm would slow down when I needed it to and pick back up when the time was right.

Our time overseas was unique to us, and the Lord has used it for our good. I pray you have enjoyed being on this journey with me. While I can never predict what your journey in life and missions will bring, I hope you feel more equipped to handle the logistic elements you may face and that being more familiar with some of the spiritual aspects will bring you freedom. Finally, I pray that you would picture yourself as that woman in the field, and as you begin your life of living uprooted, you would stay rooted in Christ and stay in tune with the composition you and God are writing together and enjoy the dance.

Let me pray for you.

Prayer:

Father God, as we close out this chapter of my story, I pray those who have traveled with me through this book would be blessed by what I've shared and that these experiences will help prepare them for their own journey. I pray you would walk with them and give them strength and wisdom to grow and learn through their experiences. I also pray that their stories would help those who come after them.

Our story is not over. I pray as we move forward that I may learn even more from you and perhaps have the opportunity to share our future adventures. Until then, let's keep dancing.

Endnotes

[1] Brain and Spine Team, "The Science Is Clear: Why Multitasking Doesn't Work," Health Essentials from Cleveland Clinic (Health Essentials from Cleveland Clinic, March 10, 2021), https://health.clevelandclinic.org/science-clear-multitasking-doesnt-work/.

[2] Kendra Cherry, "7 Useful Tips for Improving Your Mental Focus," Verywell Mind, September 17, 2020, https://www.verywellmind.com/things-you-can-do-to-improve-your-mental-focus-4115389.

[3] "The Top 10 Causes of Death," World Health Organization (World Health Organization, December 9, 2020), https://www.who.int/news-room/fact-sheets/detail/the-top-10-causes-of-death#:~:text=The%20world's%20biggest%20killer%20is,8.9%20million%20deaths%20in%202019.

[4] Neil T. Anderson and Timothy M. Warner, The Essential Guide to Spiritual Warfare: Learn to Use Spiritual Weapons; Keep Your Mind and Heart Strong in Christ; Recognize Satan's Lies; and Defend Your Loved Ones (Baker Publishing Group. Kindle Edition), 16.

[5] Neil T. Anderson and Timothy M. Warner, *The Essential Guide to Spiritual Warfare: Learn to Use Spiritual Weapons; Keep Your Mind and Heart Strong in Christ; Recognize Satan's Lies; and Defend Your Loved Ones* (Baker Publishing Group. Kindle Edition), 25–26.

Stay in Touch

To know more about Mari and to read more of her encouragement for missionary wives, visit her website at www.marieygabroad.com. Here Mari offers devotions and blog posts, answering questions not addressed in this book about missionary life. She also offers ideas for family connection, especially at the holidays. Connect with Mari on Facebook at https://web.facebook.com/marieygabroad or more snippets of encouragement.

ORDER INFORMATION

To order additional copies of this book, please visit
www.redemption-press.com.
Also available on Amazon.com and BarnesandNoble.com
or by calling toll-free 1-844-2REDEEM.